Hearth & Home

The Story of the Welsh House

Hearth & Home

The Story of the Welsh House

by
Paul R. Davis

Logaston Press

LOGASTON PRESS
Little Logaston Woonton Almeley
Herefordshire HR3 6QH
logastonpress.co.uk

First published by Logaston Press 2009
Copyright © Paul R. Davis 2009

ISBN 978 1 906663 08 7

Typeset by Logaston Press
and printed in Great Britain by
Bell & Bain Ltd., Glasgow

Illustrations on front cover, clockwise from top left:
Nantwallter (St Fagans); Talgarth (Trefeglwys); Sker House (Porthcawl);
Llwyncelyn (Cwmyoy); Llanerch y Cawr (Rhaeadr); Plas Mawr (Conwy)
Rear cover from top to bottom:
Gwydir Castle (Llanrwst); St Fagans Castle (Cardiff); Great House (Monmouth)
Illustration on p.iii: Ty Hwnt y Bwlch, Cwmyoy, an upland long-house

Contents

To Paige and Kristopher,
in the hope they find more wonders in the countryside than on a computer screen

Penarth (Newtown) is an H-plan house probably dating from the sixteenth century. The closely spaced and diagonal framing was particularly popular in the Tudor period

Acknowledgements

Many thanks are due to the numerous householders up and down the country who have allowed me to draw, measure, photograph and rummage around their historic houses over the past ten years or so. Thanks also to various individuals in CADW, the National Trust, the National Monument Record for Wales and the National Museum of Wales. In particular I would like to thank Suzanne Allen (Llancaiach Fawr), Richard Suggett (RCAHMW), and Dr Gerallt Nash (National History Museum, St Fagans) for allowing me access to survey and photograph various buildings at St Fagans. In addition my deep appreciation goes to Mr Peter Smith for correspondence and useful advice over recent years, and of course for enriching our knowledge of the Welsh house.

All the illustrations belong to the author, apart from those on pages *xi* and 43, which are reproduced with the kind permission of the RCAHMW.

The storeyed porch was a particularly imposing development of the Renaissance style in Wales, adding grace and grandeur to even the smallest house. This impressive example is the Old Vicarage at Berriew (Powys) dated 1616

Ty Mawr, Castle Caereinion, built around 1460. All the internal partition walls are aisled box-frames, but the hall itself is spanned by a huge base-cruck seen in part in the foreground

Plas yn Pentre, a timber-framed house near Llangollen, built on the site of a monastic grange. The porch and dormer windows are typically elaborate Renaissance features added to the building in 1634

Introduction

There are enough manor houses and farmhouses and cottages in Wales still to show us
that there was almost instinctively in the builders of these a natural taste for what was
fitting and pleasurable and beautiful.

T.E. Ellis (1897)

Just over two hundred years ago, when the countryside of Wales had yet to be transformed by the heavy hand of industry and the capital city of Cardiff was little more than a village, an English academic and cleric by the name of William Coxe made a slow and weary trek through the mountains of Monmouthshire. Coxe was just one of many travellers at this time who published travelogues and semi-poetical guidebooks chronicling their adventures in search of the 'romantic' landscape of Wild Wales. Aside from the natural wonders of the region, its mountains and valleys, historic monuments and picturesque half-forgotten hamlets, Coxe also spared a few florid strokes of his pen to recall the simple homes of the rural folk he encountered on his way. He was one of the very few to do so, for the majority of the artists, writers and poets scrambling over Wales at this time only had eyes for the country's more obvious architectural relics – the towering ruins of ivy-clad castles, the gothic grandeur of shattered monasteries, the quaint parish churches, and the mysterious 'Druidical' stone monuments. It was these antiquities that drew the praise and admiration of the early visitor, and rarely was any time spared for the humble house. It was only much later that the architectural and social importance of the Welsh house was appreciated; but by then the very traditions that had given birth to and nurtured such distinctive buildings had passed away.

This is a book about those houses, about the homes built by the inhabitants of Wales from the earliest times almost up to the present day. It does not explore the castles and palaces of the ruling elite, nor the stately homes of the rich and famous; it examines the traditional or vernacular dwellings of the middle and lower classes.

In this context the term 'traditional' means buildings constructed by the age-old method of transmitting ideas by word of mouth and by skills passed from master to apprentice through the generations. Traditional buildings were made by local craftsmen using familiar styles and techniques, rather than by trained architects following academic guidelines. Throughout the centuries, the mountainous interior of Wales proved to be a hindrance to the rapid spread of new concepts from the urban centres of civilisation'. Isolated rural communities thus retained their familiar customs far longer than other areas of Britain.

1

Before the middle of the nineteenth century it was difficult and costly to transport building materials from one part of the country to another and craftsmen had to use whatever could be obtained locally. These buildings are therefore characteristic of the region in which they are situated and share features rarely encountered outside that area. The term 'vernacular' simply refers to everyday, commonplace structures rather than grander buildings such as castles, churches, cathedrals, stately homes and the like.

Within these broad definitions there exist many types of traditional buildings constructed from a variety of materials. A clay-walled thatched cottage dating from 1840 is a vernacular building, while a contemporary brick terraced house is not; similarly a manor house of 1500 could be viewed as 'traditional' in a way that a nearby castle (built some two centuries earlier) would not be. To take a more detailed example of this kind of distinction, imagine that a moderately wealthy farmer of the 1600s has accrued sufficient money to set about rebuilding his dilapidated ancestral home. The local craftsman given the task would obtain stone from a nearby quarry and oak from an adjacent forest. With these raw materials he would create a dwelling to a certain size and layout in the style that he, and other builders of the area, had been constructing for previous generations. At the same time, the rich owner of the surrounding estate might also embark on a rebuilding programme. He would be more likely to employ the services of a professional architect familiar with all the current trends in interior designs and architectural fashions, and could afford to import expensive building materials from outside the region to give his home extra glamour. Thus two houses, built around the same time and in the same locality,

Alltybella, near Usk, a cruck-framed hall with a Renaissance tower block added in 1599

could be quite different. The modest 'home-made' farmhouse is a vernacular building, while the grander mansion belongs to the realms of 'polite' architecture.

Of course, nothing is quite as clear-cut as this: traditional buildings sometimes sport features normally found in upper-class houses, and many outwardly classical buildings may be thinly disguised vernacular structures. It is also important to appreciate that most of the traditional houses still standing did not belong to the 'common people'. For much of our history, the majority of the population was poor, scraping a living on meagre plots of unprofitable land. Their houses were so insubstantial that the passage of time (coupled with the wind and rain) has brought about their decay over a relatively short period. Take for example the mud-walled thatched cottages, once a common sight in rural areas. A number still survive, much patched up and modernised, but the majority have disappeared and are now commemorated by archive photographs. The cottages depicted in these historic prints may look ancient, but in reality few would have been built much before 1800. The buildings we think of as vernacular are generally quite substantial works constructed by middle-class farmers and well-to-do landowners. The older a surviving house, the greater the likelihood that it was built by someone of high social standing, for the simple reason that they could afford to build dwellings of substance.

In Wales, the lifespan of traditional buildings fits more or less neatly into the four centuries between 1400 and 1800. During the early years of the nineteenth century, building in the vernacular declined due to the availability of architectural pattern books

A town house in Ruthin with later rendering masking almost all of the elaborate timber framing

3

and the introduction of cheap mass-produced materials into all parts of the country by the burgeoning transportation system; while domestic buildings built before 1400 are mostly represented by ruins and archaeological sites. These nonetheless are covered by this book, to show how the story of the Welsh house began, and how the earliest inhabitants of Wales kept the rain off their heads.

Interest in the traditional houses of Wales is a comparatively recent phenomenon. Apart from occasional brief references in antiquarian and historical guidebooks, articles on vernacular buildings only began to appear in learned journals towards the end of the nineteenth century and it was not until the early years of the twentieth century that interest really began to grow. The first publication to explore the humbler forms of architecture was *The Old Cottages of Snowdonia* (1908) by Harold Hughes and Herbert North. This charming little book illustrates the small houses found in abundance in the uplands of north Wales, and reveals how such modest dwellings have an intrinsic value of their own.

The first book to deal with native houses on a countrywide basis was *The Welsh House* (1940) by Iorwerth Peate. This publication enshrined years of fieldwork carried out at a time when the age-old way of life in the Welsh countryside was rapidly changing to meet the demands of modern agriculture and traditional buildings were increasingly being abandoned, destroyed or renovated out of all recognition. Within a few years of the book's appearance the Welsh Folk Museum (now the National History Museum) was established at St Fagans near Cardiff, with Peate as its first curator. Peate's broad overview of native architecture was soon complemented by the three volumes of *Monmouthshire Houses* (1951-

Downs Cross, Llantwit Major, a seventeenth-century house of medieval origin

54) by Sir Cyril Fox and Lord Raglan. This groundbreaking work made extensive use of plans, drawings and photographs to explore the development and regional characteristics of houses in one particular corner of Wales. The foundation of the Vernacular Archaeology Group in 1954 was another boost to the study and preservation of traditional buildings.

The responsibility for recording the archaeological heritage of Britain has long been the preserve of the Royal Commission on Ancient and Historical Monuments. The department concerned with Wales (hereafter referred to as RCAHMW) had published county inventories before the First World War, but only the 'big' houses got a mention. Things soon began to change. Domestic architecture made an appearance in the Anglesey Inventory (1937) and formed a substantial portion of the Caernarfonshire set (1956-64). By the time the Commissioners explored the building heritage of Glamorgan in the 1980s, two hefty volumes were needed to cover the houses surveyed! But of all the books published on this subject so far, one stands out; Peter Smith's *Houses of the Welsh Countryside* (1975, revised version 1988) is the most detailed survey of regional architecture yet published, and is likely to remain the last word in vernacular studies for many years to come.

And so on to this book. There are thousands of houses built before 1800 scattered across Wales. Some are rapidly falling into ruin, others have long been so; a great many have undergone modernisation to such an extent that it would take an expert to detect their original structures. Those that have survived relatively unchanged since they were built are rare indeed.

Of the great number of early houses that do survive (in whatever state) only a small percentage are accessible to the public, and this book tells you where to find them. It is divided into three sections covering the main historical periods of traditional architecture. The first section deals with prehistoric and Roman houses that still exist in the form of archaeological sites, the second section surveys the domestic buildings surviving from the Middle Ages, and the third part covers houses built after the Reformation, when the old medieval halls were adapted or abandoned in favour of new plans and ideas.

Any house mentioned in the text which is accessible to the public appears in **bold type** and is included in the list of places to visit at the end of each section. The list includes information about access and opening times; the details were correct at the time of writing, but it might be advisable to check in advance of a visit. Please remember that any other site referred to (or illustrated) is privately owned and its inclusion here does not mean there is a right of access. Place-name spellings are taken from the most recent editions of the Ordnance Survey (OS) maps. At the end of this book there is a section giving information on properties with limited access or where an appointment to visit must be made with the owners in advance. For further information on these, and other houses in Wales, you may wish to consult the listed buildings records kept by the regional councils and CADW, the organisation responsible for historic buildings in Wales. The main source for further information on historic buildings is the National Monuments Record for Wales. This extensive photographic and documentary archive is housed in the offices of the RCAHMW and can be consulted by research students and members of the public.

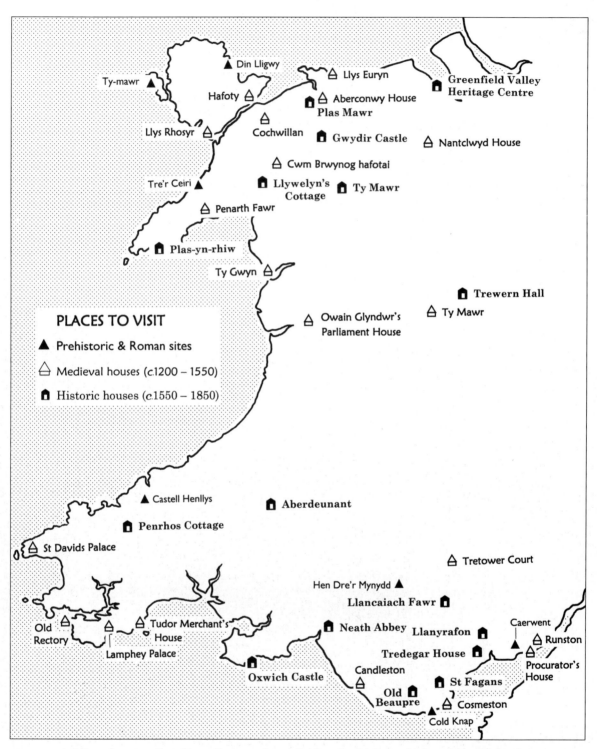

Ty-mawr ▲
Din Lligwy ▲
Hafoty ⌂
Llys Euryn ⌂
Greenfield Valley Heritage Centre ⌂
Aberconwy House ⌂
Plas Mawr ⌂
Llys Rhosyr ⌂
Cochwillan ⌂
Gwydir Castle ⌂
Nantclwyd House ⌂
Cwm Brwynog hafotai ⌂
Tre'r Ceiri ▲
Llywelyn's Cottage ⌂
Ty Mawr ⌂
Penarth Fawr ⌂
Plas-yn-rhiw ⌂
Ty Gwyn ⌂
Trewern Hall ⌂
Ty Mawr ⌂
Owain Glyndwr's Parliament House ⌂

PLACES TO VISIT

▲ Prehistoric & Roman sites

⌂ Medieval houses (*c.*1200 – 1550)

⌂ Historic houses (*c.*1550 – 1850)

Castell Henllys ▲
Aberdeunant ⌂
Penrhos Cottage ⌂
St Davids Palace ⌂
Tretower Court ⌂
Hen Dre'r Mynydd ▲
Llancaiach Fawr ⌂
Caerwent
Old Rectory ⌂
Tudor Merchant's House ⌂
Neath Abbey ⌂
Llanyrafon ⌂
Runston ⌂
Lamphey Palace
Tredegar House ⌂
Procurator's House ⌂
Oxwich Castle ⌂
Candleston ⌂
St Fagans ⌂
Old Beaupre ⌂
Cosmeston ⌂
Cold Knap ▲

Map showing the places that can be visited and which are featured in this book

PART ONE
4000 BC - AD 500

Beginnings

Where does the story of the Welsh house begin? With the windy rock shelters tenanted by hardy cavemen as far back as 250,000 BC, or with the animal-skin tents erected by nomadic hunters eight thousand years ago? If a house is defined as a structure built for dwelling in, natural caves do not count, although Wales has troglodyte hovels aplenty. But perhaps the question should really be – when does the story of the house *in* Wales begin? Although the culture we recognise as 'Welsh' only developed within the last few millennia, people have been living in this part of the world far longer. A quarter of a million years ago our earliest residents used the limestone escarpments of the Vale of Clwyd as a refuge while on foraging expeditions in the surrounding countryside. The cold dark reaches of Bontnewydd Cave, overlooking the river valley of the Elwy, sheltered a group of the now-extinct Neanderthal race. A few archaeological finds preserved beneath layers of mud and stalagmite are all that we have to record the existence of what must have been a tiny population struggling to live in a harsh environment.

Over an unimaginably vast period of time, the land that would eventually become known as Wales was buried under extensions of the North Polar ice cap as the global temperature fluctuated. Even during this long Ice Age there were several periods of milder climate that broke the harsh grip of the cold and enabled a few tribes to push north in search of food. They hunted animals such as mammoth, woolly rhinoceros and elk, and huddled together for warmth and shelter in the mouths of limestone caves. The meagre scraps of their lives were left behind as debris to be recovered millennia later by archaeologists at sites such as Longhole and Paviland Caves (Gower), Hoyle's Mouth (Tenby) and King Arthur's Cave (near Monmouth). These durable natural homes were used by nomadic family groups on and off for centuries, not just for living in but also for preserving the remains of their dead. Undoubtedly they also made use of temporary campsites, but all evidence for such flimsy structures has been swept away by the great environmental changes that transformed the landscape.

Around 25,000 BC the climate deteriorated again and the onset of another cold snap rendered the country virtually uninhabitable for the next fifteen thousand years. When the temperature began to rise again, the huge expanse of ice melted and shrank northwards, leaving a scarred and barren tundra-like landscape to be slowly reclaimed by creeping greenery. As the trees came back, so the vast amounts of water released by the thaw caused a fairly

Paviland Cave

rapid rise in sea level and the flooding of extensive tracts of low-lying land. By 7000 BC the rising waters had cut through the straits of Dover and transformed what had been a corner of Europe into the British Isles. This new wilderness was exploited by wandering family groups termed 'hunter-gatherers' because that is what they did. Food was gathered wherever it could be found: fish from the rivers and lakes; shellfish from the coasts; nuts, berries and fruit harvested from the bushes and wild animals such as deer, elk and boar, hunted in the great forests.

These people followed their mobile larder around, moving on once they had depleted the resources of a particular area. No metals were known at this distant period and so any tool had to be made from stone, wood, or bone. It is through the discovery of such implements that we know what little we do about these long-gone people. At a few places used as campsites archaeologists have found slight traces of tent-like dwellings, held together by thin branches stuck into the ground; insubstantial to us perhaps, but aptly suited to their needs. To picture this lifestyle we need only think of the familiar image of native American Indians living in wigwam settlements and hunting great beasts on the endless plains.

The nomadic culture of the Stone Age tribes lasted virtually unchanged for thousands of years until farming practices were adopted. There is a debate as to whether Neolithic immigrants arrived around 4000 BC and brought with them a rudimentary method of farming, whether the idea simply spread from the continent, or whether the advent of farming was a combination of the two. In any event, it was to have a profound effect on the native culture and society of Britain. A basic agricultural system of stock rearing, sowing and harvesting crops, managing the natural landscape for food production, meant that there was no need to move continually in search of food. The origins of our farming community began in the Neolithic period and – more importantly for the story of the Welsh house – these early settlers, tied to the land, began to build more permanent homesteads.

It is unlikely that the nomadic lifestyle came to an abrupt halt overnight. There is some evidence to suggest that the hunter-gatherers were not averse to staying put if the circumstances were right. Archaeologists have discovered a round house at Howick on the Northumberland coast dating from about 7600 BC, which remained in use for several generations, perhaps for more than a century. Future excavations may shed more light on the origins of fixed society in Britain.

All across Wales, the Neolithic farmers busily exploited the countryside and defined territories in order to control the available resources. The farmer has to plan in advance, when to plough and sow, when to harvest, how much grain to use, how much to store for next year's crop, which animals to kill for food and which to keep for breeding. The time and labour invested in the daily toil, and the painstaking task of clearing the scrub and undergrowth with stone axes, effectively gave them possession of the land they cleared. Leading a more static lifestyle, the Neolithic farmers built more durable habitations than had been the norm before, and went to the trouble of constructing massive stone burial chambers to house the remains of their honoured dead, so that in a way their ancestors had a stake in the claim to the local land. These tombs are now the most lasting and obvious relics of the Neolithic peoples in Wales and Western Europe. Who can fail to be impressed by the raw sculptural qualities of the megalithic constructions still standing at Bryn Celli Ddu (Anglesey), Pentre Ifan (Pembrokeshire) and Tinkinswood (Cardiff)? But unlike these ancient mortuaries, the homes of the living have disappeared without a trace. Just as a glorious medieval cathedral survives to this day while the timber buildings that once clustered around it have not, so in Neolithic times the simple houses have crumbled away, leaving only the more durable stone monuments behind. It has only been through modern excavations of more prominent ancient sites that evidence of Neolithic houses has been found.

For example, one of the oldest houses in Wales was discovered in 1943 by archaeologists digging on a natural volcanic outcrop known as Clegyr Boia, close to St Davids Cathedral. They were excavating a small settlement of Iron Age date (c.600 BC to 100 AD), when they stumbled across the remains of a much older structure. Within a sheltered hollow near the summit they found a series of holes cut into the bedrock, marking the position of upright timber posts. Although the posts had long since decayed away, the remaining pattern of holes indicated that a building of roughly rectangular plan had stood here. It measured around 7m long by 4m wide and probably had walls constructed from upright poles interlaced with branches, reinforced at the base with stone rubble and turf clods. The position of the entrance was marked by a simple gap in the foundations. A row of four posts supported the central ridgepole, on which lesser rafters were set to complete

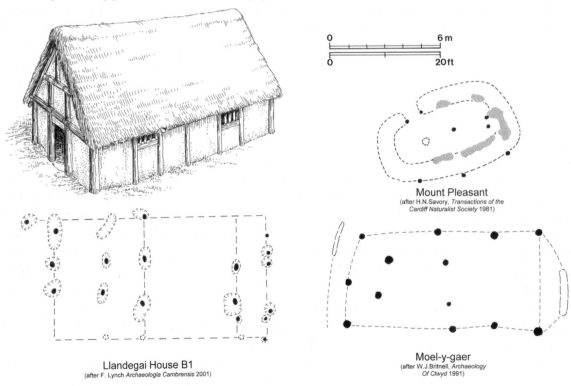

0   6 m

0   20 ft

Mount Pleasant
(after H.N.Savory, *Transactions of the
Cardiff Naturalist Society* 1981)

Llandegai House B1
(after F. Lynch *Archaeologia Cambrensis* 2001)

Moel-y-gaer
(after W.J.Britnell, *Archaeology
Of Clwyd* 1991)

Reconstruction and plans of Neolithic house sites

a crude framework roofed over with turf or thatch. The rear slope of the roof rested on the outcropping rock. The occupants would probably have slept on a simple bed covered with straw or bracken. There was no fireplace inside the building and any cooking would have been carried out in a hearth-pit discovered nearby. The archaeologists also found slighter traces of a second hut a short distance away. These simple dwellings were home to a small farming family who lived on this isolated, windswept crag sometime between five and six thousand years ago.

In the 1960s another Neolithic house site was discovered during a rescue excavation carried out in advance of redevelopment at Llandegai on the outskirts of Bangor. Again, all that remained of the dwelling was a series of post-holes, cut into the ground and packed with stone rubble to hold the vanished timbers. The pattern of holes indicated that a larger and more substantial house stood here, measuring about 13m long by at least 6m wide, with a roof supported by two parallel rows of upright posts. The interior seems to have been divided into three unequally sized chambers. The central compartment was used as the main living space and was probably warmed by an open hearth (although disturbance to the ground had removed the vital archaeological evidence to confirm this). The outer walls had also suffered from later damage, but it is thought they may have been constructed either from upright planks or small posts interlaced with branches.

Dating evidence suggests that the Llandegai house was occupied in an early phase of the Neolithic period, sometime between 4500 and 3900 BC and was eventually burned down. Several centuries later the surrounding area was reused as a religious and ceremonial centre (though whether the choice of site was deliberate or coincidental it is now impossible to prove). More recent excavations carried out by the Gwynedd Archaeological Trust have revealed the site of a second Neolithic house at Llandegai. The remains uncovered so far indicate a substantial timber post-built dwelling comparable in size and age to the previously discovered site.

Another setting of postholes unearthed in the 1970s at Moel-y-gaer hillfort (near Flint) may represent the outlines of an oblong building, 10m by 5m, built around 3000 BC. More fragmentary remains of Neolithic dwelling sites have also been found at Gwernvale near Brecon, and on the bleak moors of Cefn Glas above the Rhondda Valley. At the former site a setting of holes beneath the remains of a later burial chamber marked a long-vanished timber building 5.5m wide by at least 10m long. The Rhondda site was represented by an arrangement of stones at the upper end of a hut about 3m wide by just over 9m long. Presumably the walls were constructed from layers of turf or clay resting on rubble foundations. Two hearths were found on the earthen floor, which is rather unusual and may indicate that the remains are actually two smaller buildings set end to end rather than one long one. Such snug, smelly hovels were to represent the normal domestic residence for the majority of Welshmen for the next six thousand years.

The remains of similar rectangular timber and earth houses have been found outside Wales, proving that such buildings were the most anyone could expect in home comforts during the Stone Age. However, far to the north in the windswept Orkney Islands, the discovery of a substantial settlement revealed that people of this age had the technology and skill to build dwellings on an almost palatial scale. At Skara Brae the excavated houses have well-built stone walls, central hearths, box-like bed cavities, in-house toilets and even dressers for displaying prized possessions. Because of the scarcity of timber on the islands everything was built from durable stone and this factor, coupled with a sandstorm that buried everything under a protective shroud, has left us the finest example of Neolithic domestic architecture in Britain.

The Bronze and Iron Ages

In the course of the third millennium BC, knowledge of metalworking reached Britain from the continent and more effective implements, cast at first from copper and then bronze, gradually supplanted the ubiquitous stone tools. With better equipment the early farmers could clear away dense scrub and woodland far more efficiently than before, bringing more land under cultivation and producing a surplus of food. This in turn led to a rise in population and the development of a wealthier and more complex society. The Bronze Age (*c.*2300 BC to 600 BC) is characterised by an increase in ritual and funerary monuments such as standing stones, circles and burial mounds. It was during this period that the great megalithic rings at Stonehenge and Avebury were constructed, along with the many smaller Welsh examples still to be seen at Gors Fawr (Preseli), Cerrig Duon (Glyntawe) and Penmaenmawr.

In Glamorgan alone, four burial mounds (including the site at Mount Pleasant illustrated on p.10) have been found upon excavation to overlie earlier dwelling sites, while in Pembrokeshire ritual stone monuments at Stackpole and Rhos y Clegyrn (Fishguard) were built on top of older huts. Was this re-use of a dwelling site pure coincidence, or was there a reason for it? Might it be that the builders felt it necessary to erect a monument over a house to provide the interred person with a dwelling in the afterlife?

During the early phase of the Bronze Age the oblong houses of the Neolithic period

Hut settlement at Hen Dre'r Mynydd (Blaenrhondda)

gave way to huts of circular plan and for the next two thousand years native houses were predominately built 'in the round'. Why this happened is far from clear – one would think that a square house with a ridged roof would be easier to build than a round one, given the limited means and equipment then available – but perhaps there was a more subtle reason for the change. Since the hearth was the centre point of family life, around which everyone huddled to keep warm during the cold months of the year, then a circular building with a central fire would be the most convenient and economic means of distributing the heat evenly.

The change in shape was soon accompanied by a radical shift in settlement patterns. Whereas the evidence for Neolithic and early-Bronze Age communities suggests that people mainly lived in scattered, isolated farmsteads, after 1000 BC settlements began to appear on hills and high ground, protected by timber stockades and earthwork ramparts. The reason for the sudden proliferation of hillforts and defended enclosures throughout Britain is still a matter of debate and several factors may be responsible. At this time there was an influx of Celtic tribes from Europe who brought with them a more formidable metal for use as tools and weapons – iron. There was also a marked deterioration in the climate, leading to greater exploitation of the available land and natural resources. More importantly, there is the human propensity for violence which seems to be the inevitable side effect of a developing hierarchical society. Whatever the explanation, hillforts were evidently considered a necessary part of life, and it was from this Age of Iron that the earliest houses in Wales started to emerge.

Hillforts are found throughout the country and one of the finest examples is **Tre'r Ceiri** on the Lleyn peninsula in north Wales. The defences and dwellings of the fort were constructed from local stone rubble and are particularly well preserved. Within the massive ramparts can be seen over 150 round houses, varying between 3m and 8m across, marked by clusters of circular foundations. Some are freestanding, others lean against the defensive walls, but the majority are linked together to form long chains of huts – perhaps an early experiment in terraced housing? No wonder local people once thought the hill was the dwelling place of giants, as the Welsh name suggests.

The neighbouring peaks of Garn Boduan and Carn Fadryn are similarly covered in numerous huts, implying large and thriving local communities. What cannot be answered at present is whether these seemingly impregnable (but challengingly exposed) mountaintops were permanently occupied, or just refuges for the local populace in times of unrest. Nor can we be certain that every hut was occupied at any one time. Some of the massively defended hillforts were surely designed as tribal strongholds, but the majority of the slighter earthworks must represent the remains of small farmsteads and family holdings.

Outline of a round house at Tre'r Ceiri hillfort

Reconstructed Iron Age round house at Castell Henllys near Cardigan

And it is clear from the many scattered hut groups and associated field enclosures that not everyone chose to live inside fortifications.

The information gleaned from various excavations and surviving remains enables us to picture a typical round house of the period. The external appearance is easily envisaged: a low circular wall almost hidden by the overhanging eaves of the great shaggy thatched roof rising to the sky in a sweeping cone. The entrance was simply a gap in the wall, usually positioned on the side away from the prevailing wind and sometimes protected by a small porch. Within lay a single spacious living chamber as much as 12m across. Close to the encircling wall where the headroom was low, light wattle screens may have been used to partition off store or sleeping areas. The rest of the interior would be used for general day-to-day living, cooking, weaving and craftworking, all focused around the warming hearth in the middle of the house. Some of the smoke from the fire would have escaped through the open door (there were no windows), but most fumes wafted into the high roof space and seeped out through the thatch. The heavier industrial work and metal smelting might be carried out in a separate hut. No round house survives in anything like its original form today, but reconstructed examples can be seen at the **National History Museum** (St Fagans), and **Castell Henllys** (near Cardigan).

The use of stone aids the longevity of a building, so where there is an abundance of this material prehistoric round houses can be seen as circular rings of tumbled boulders, usually swathed in grass and bracken. In other parts of the country they were constructed from wood and have consequently not survived. To make a timber house, a builder would set up a ring of stout upright posts marking the outer perimeter wall, and fill the gaps between each post with a wattle-work of flexible twigs. Over this would be smeared a sticky mix of clay and straw (the original version of our modern wall plaster), which dried to form a hard and fairly waterproof casing. This ancient technique is known as *wattle and daub* and it remained an important element of timber-framed buildings until comparatively recent times. Timber buildings may seem insubstantial, but with regular repair it is thought that a large round house could have lasted up to fifty years. However, unlike stone buildings a timber house will decay rapidly once it is abandoned and will leave virtually no visible trace above ground.

Only in waterlogged soil does timber have any chance of surviving the centuries. Recent exploration of the marshlands bordering the Severn estuary between Cardiff and Caldicot has brought to light a wealth of wooden structures preserved beneath thick layers of tidal mud. This area is reckoned to be the richest coastal archaeological site in Britain. Since 1990, the remains of wooden buildings of Bronze and Iron Age date have been found here, as well as interconnecting trackways, ancient tree stumps and eight thousand year-old human footprints. At Goldcliff (Newport), the blackened stumps of timbers jutting up through the mud led archaeologists to the remains of at least seven buildings, dating from between 593 and 272 BC. The best-preserved structure measured 8.4m by 5.6m and had walls formed of close-set upright planks. Aside from the excellent state of preservation, the most remarkable feature of the site is that all the buildings are rectangular, in total contrast to the commonplace round houses of the period. A few other oblong Iron Age buildings have been found in this part of the country, raising the possibility that there was a regional preference for this type of structure. However, it is perhaps unlikely that the Goldcliff buildings were purely domestic, since no hearths were found inside. The presence of cattle tracks in the mud suggests that the settlement was only occupied during the summer months by farmers exploiting the coastal pastures.

Roman Residences

Barely two thousand years ago a sweeping change in British society and culture was initiated by the abrupt arrival of the Romans. In the process of greedily expanding their empire throughout the known world, they conquered lowland Britain in the years following AD 43; but like other invaders after them, they found Wales a tougher nut to crack. By the time of the invasion, Wales had been divided into at least six territories ruled by native tribes, principally the Demetae, Deceangli, Ordovices and Silures. The Roman historian Tacitus records that thirteen military campaigns were launched against these tribes between the years AD 47 and 77 before they were effectively subdued and the mountainous countryside was ringed by a network of roads and military bases.

Having eventually brought the Celts to their knees, the Romans set about imposing the benefits of civilised life. Towns were established to entice the locals down from their windswept hillforts and provide economic stability to a conquered territory. Consumer goods, coins, imported pottery and luxury foodstuffs made their gradual appearance in the economy. They also brought with them a new language, which remained in use in some form or other long after their Empire had passed into oblivion. Our modern word 'domestic' for instance, derives from the Latin *domus* (house).

The design of Roman buildings did not evolve from a local tradition, of course, but was imported directly into Britain. Roman builders worked with a wide variety of materials and mixed them to create bricks, roofing tiles, and even that most familiar of modern substances, concrete. Their houses consisted of small square rooms linked together to form long rows, often arranged around a small courtyard and accessed from an internal corridor or an external veranda. The idea was to provide a shady retreat from the hot Mediterranean sun, but in these wetter lands the enclosed courtyards must have been rather damp and gloomy.

Unlike the communal multi-purpose round house of the Celts, each room in a Roman building had its own function and the more important would have been graced with all the comforts that the empire could provide and the owner could afford. Most of the floors would be laid with bricks, tiles or *opus signinum* (a smooth layer of cement and crushed brick), while the very important rooms would have intricate mosaic patterns created from tiny blocks of coloured stone set in mortar. Whether the walls were stone or timber-framed, they would be plastered and painted in a fashion we might today find intolerably garish. Rectangular panels of bright red, ochre and black were popular, as were imitation stonework, floral motifs and countryside scenes.

Portable braziers were commonly used to warm the rooms, but people with enough money could opt for the ultimate in home luxuries – an underfloor heating system (*hypocaust*). This advanced, yet very simple, method worked by having floors raised on stone pillars

so that hot air from an adjacent furnace could circulate through the space and warm up the surface. The rising fumes would pass through ceramic ducts embedded in the walls to give an extra bit of 'central heating'. The same system was used to fuel another important piece of domestic luxury, a bath suite. This was not a bath in the modern sense of the word, but more like a combined sauna, gymnasium and social meeting place. Upper-class Romans took their ablutions seriously, and a visit to the baths could last several hours.

A typical Roman living room,
reconstructed at Fishbourne (Sussex)

There are no Roman houses surviving intact in Britain today; all we can see are the preserved foundations revealed through excavations. The heavy military presence in Wales means that most of the remains on display are forts and army bases such as *Isca* (Caerleon), and *Segontium* (Caernarfon). The first bases were hurriedly constructed from timber and only gradually were the buildings replaced in stone. This is not the context in which to explore such forts in detail, but it is worth noting that they were invariably built to a well-established plan. Within a rectangular enclosure stood row upon row of barrack blocks, with the *praetorium* (commander's house) occupying the central area. In style and layout this would closely resemble ordinary domestic houses and it would undoubtedly have been better finished than the spartan quarters the rank and file had to put up with. Outside the fort gates a civilian settlement (*vicus*) usually grew up, sometimes outliving the military base it served. Cardiff, Cowbridge, Monmouth and Usk, for instance, probably originated as garrison towns.

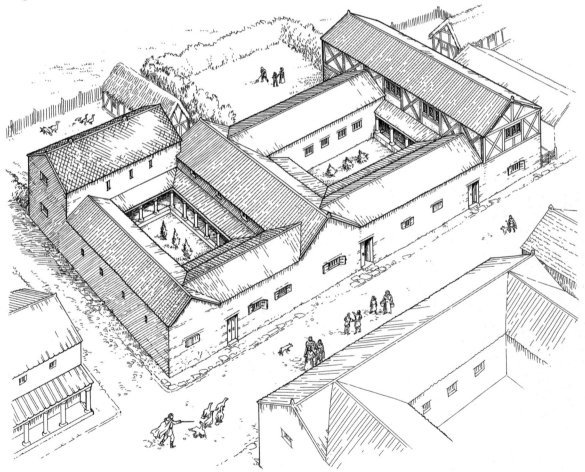

Reconstruction of the double courtyard house at Pound Lane, Caerwent. Since only foundations remain, many of the details are conjectural, but the drawing shows the range of styles and materials used in the Roman town

Purely domestic Roman remains are much scarcer in Wales, but there is a very important site called *Venta Silurum* ('the market town of the Silures'), now known as **Caerwent**. This was established late in the first century AD as a regional capital for the local Silures tribe and since the main army base was only a short distance away at Caerleon, any potential trouble could be dealt with swiftly. The new town was located on a low hill close to the Severn estuary and was at first little more than a collection of wooden buildings strung out along the main Gloucester road. In the second century AD the urban development really took off and an eighteen-hectare enclosure was established, divided up into a chessboard pattern of building plots. The main civic buildings, including the market place (*forum*) and council hall (*basilica*), occupied pride of place in the central plot. Close by, a temple took care of spiritual needs, while a large bathhouse catered for the body.

The foundations of some houses and shops in the western part of Caerwent have been excavated and preserved for posterity. As in today's towns, the most valuable commercial land was concentrated along the main street, so the buildings had to be adapted to fit into the limited space. Two second century 'strip houses' can be seen, the stone foundations outlining long and narrow buildings extending back from the street, hence the name. The large room at the front is believed to have been a blacksmith's forge, while the living quarters were crammed in behind. Early in the third century, both strip houses were modified; then a century later they were completely rebuilt and given an ornamental portico along the frontage. The main chamber was still used as a forge, which strongly suggests a long-running family business.

Away from the prime retail area there was less pressure on available land and the builders could opt for more spacious dwellings. Numerous courtyard houses were found in excavations carried out here in the late-nineteenth century. One very large building near the southern gateway was interpreted as an inn or hostelry. All the remains were subsequently covered over, but fortunately the results of further archaeological work in the 1980s can still be seen in Pound Lane. Here are preserved the foundations of a large house with two internal courtyards, which dates from the early fourth century. The principal rooms were arranged around the smaller north yard and had mosaic floors, plastered and painted walls, and underfloor heating. The stone pillars that supported the raised floor of the *hypocaust* can still be seen. Even the colonnaded walkway beside the courtyard had a floor of inlaid coloured stones forming a simple but effective geometric design. As only the foundations survive today, it is uncertain if the vanished superstructure was stone or timber-framed, nor is it possible to be sure if there was an upper floor. The rooms around the larger south courtyard were much plainer and seem to have been used as agricultural stores, suggesting that this building was a sort of urban farm. Whatever its function, this twin-courtyard house must have been the seat of a fairly well to do member of the Romano-British community at Caerwent.

Another civic capital was established further west at *Moridunum* for the Demetae tribe, but the site is now occupied by modern-day Carmarthen. Elsewhere in Wales, several sites connected with Roman industrial activities have been explored. The preserved remains of a bathhouse at Prestatyn must have been associated with a mining settlement close by (and was no doubt a popular venue for sweaty off-duty labourers). The Clwyd-Powys Archaeological Trust excavated a substantial building at Pentre Farm (Flint) beside the Dee estuary in the 1970s. In about AD 120, at least three timber-framed rectangular buildings were constructed around a small courtyard containing an ornamental pool. The complex underwent considerable rebuilding and alterations in later years, including the addition of a bath suite and gatehouse, before it was dismantled in the third century. Having examined the evidence, the excavators considered that this was connected with the leadmining ventures in the locality and was probably the residence of an official.

A similar conclusion was reached about an important site unearthed on the coast at **Cold Knap** (Barry) in 1980 by the Glamorgan-Gwent Archaeological Trust. The excavated foundations have now been preserved and what can be seen is a classic example of a courtyard building dating from the third and fourth centuries AD. There are four wings of rooms ranged around a central garden, all connected by an internal veranda. Just beyond the south-west corner stood a detached square building that could be interpreted as a watchtower. Although the building plan suggests a typical country house, its position on the exposed coast and rather spartan details may mean that it had a military or civil function. Perhaps it was the residence of an official dignitary associated with a nearby port, or even a guesthouse for maritime travellers.

In England, the ultimate statement of Romanisation beyond the towns was the rural farmstead,

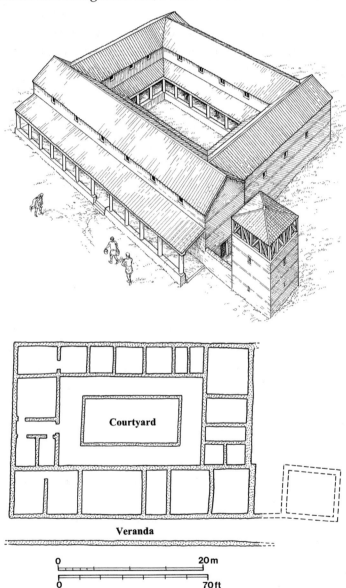

Plan and reconstruction drawing of Cold Knap, Barry. The appearance of the 'tower' is conjectural

or *villa*, built by those lucky few who had produced enough returns on their land to be able to invest in grand buildings and who chose to associate themselves with the sophisticated Mediterranean lifestyle of the ruling elite. In Wales, alas, no remains of a villa can be seen today and the few sites explored fall short of the English examples in size and quality. Excavations have taken place in Glamorgan on three villas, the largest and most elaborate of which stood at Llantwit Major. The site lies in the fertile Vale of Glamorgan, an area particularly rich in Roman-period settlements, and has been investigated by archaeologists several times in the last century and a quarter. The ground plan of a main L-shaped residential block was uncovered, along with four other buildings grouped around a courtyard (see plan below). These outbuildings were probably agricultural stores, barns, granaries and workshops, and included a large hall for the numerous servants and labourers working on the estate.

The main residential block was divided up into around twenty box-like rooms accessed from an external corridor. Most of the rooms had stone or concrete floors, but the more important ones in the north wing had mosaics of intricate coloured patterns. Part of the building had an underfloor heating system, but most rooms would have made do with braziers to keep the chill Welsh weather at bay. A few windows even had the luxury of glass. From fragments of buried plaster it was possible to deduce that the walls had been painted on at least two occasions with different designs. The earliest phase had panels or horizontal bands of dark ochre, red and black. This was superseded by an imitation marble effect of pale blue flecked with crimson. The larger room was probably the main dining chamber (*triclinium*), where the affluent owners of the villa reclined on their couches to toy with the delicacies heaped onto the central table.

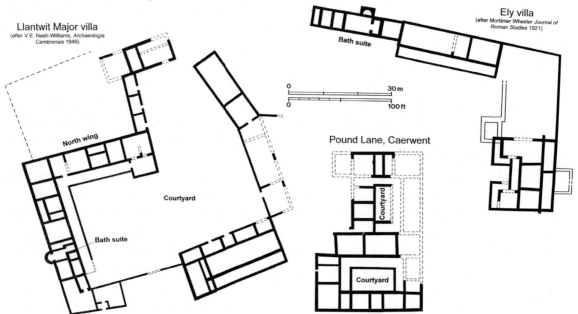

Comparative plans of Roman buildings mentioned in the text

The west wing was devoted to that uniquely Roman institution, bathing, and contained a lavish suite of rooms for the owners to indulge in the art of keeping clean. People entered the undressing room (*apodyterium*) and then proceeded to the cold room (*frigidarium*) with its semi-circular plunge pool, before passing into the warm room (*tepidarium*) and hot room (*caldarium*). The whole point of this elaborate ritual was to make the patron sweat. Servants would then massage the bathers with scented oil, mixing it into the dirt and sweat on the skin and scraping the residue away with a blunt metal scythe-like implement. Another dip in the cold pool closed the pores. All this luxury was made possible by hard-working servants keeping the furnaces blazing, and thus forcing hot air to circulate through the raised flooring and heating ducts in the walls.

Recent investigations suggest that the residential block replaced an earlier timber building and that the Llantwit villa was remodelled and extended around AD 200, following a period of neglect. The finer details of the mosaic floors were added after AD 300, shortly before the villa was abandoned. This is not quite the end of the story, because over forty human skeletons have been found here, which the excavators thought might have been the hastily buried victims of a battle.

Another substantial villa lay at Ely on the outskirts of Cardiff (see plan opposite). The main building was a compact structure with two projecting wings and a front veranda graced by a mosaic floor and a colonnade of imported stone pillars. Clearly first impressions mattered a lot to the owners. There was also a second accommodation block here, which was later provided with a bath suite. The villa was probably built early in the second century and then reconstructed after a fire in the third century, before being abandoned by AD 330.

This arrangement of two large buildings at Llantwit and Ely (presumably one for the owners and one for servants) has also been identified at Bassaleg near Newport. Although the site has not been excavated, the foundations were detected by the observation of parch-marks in the ground during aerial reconnaissance in 1996. The main residential building appears to have been a typical multi-roomed villa with a front veranda and porch, while a short distance away is an equally spacious building on a slightly different alignment. This contains three small rooms at one end of a very large hall, which had a roof supported on a double row of internal pillars. Such aisled construction is more often encountered in the great civic buildings of Roman towns.

Not all villas display such obvious foreign influence in their design. At Whitton (Llancarfan), excavations within a small earthwork enclosure showed how a Celtic hut settlement was remodelled from AD 100 onwards along typical Roman lines. Later phases of occupation included a succession of rectangular masonry buildings (or possibly timber-framed ones on stone foundations) standing within the earthwork defences. Similar discoveries of Roman-style buildings inside outwardly native enclosures have been made at Llangynog and Cwmbrwyn, near Carmarthen.

Some hillforts remained in occupation (though not as military strongholds) and it seems that for the majority of the rural population life continued much as it had for their

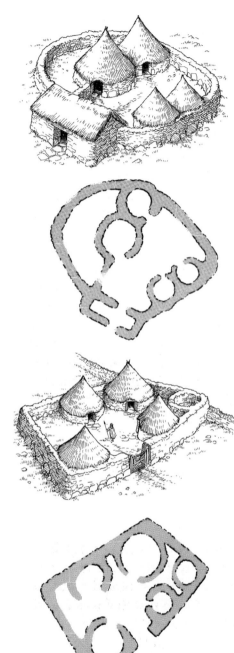

forebears, the majority of rural farmsteads being based on the older settlement patterns favoured by the Celts. The round house still dominated local architecture, but change was on the way as the disciplined, orderly mind of the Roman builder brought right angles into the curvilinear world of the Celts. In north-west Wales native farms developed into a very distinctive arrangement of round and oblong stone buildings squeezed together within a walled courtyard. At its most basic level an enclosed settlement might contain just one house and could only have been intended for a small family. More often there are two or three huts (even as many as seven), grouped within courtyards of varying size and shape. Almost three hundred examples have been recorded, but only about a dozen have been excavated. Some archaeologists believe they developed as a direct result of Roman influence, while others think they evolved out of the native building tradition due to changes in economy and climate.

The best-preserved example of this type of farmstead is **Din Lligwy** on Anglesey. Here the builders created a pentagonal-shaped courtyard enclosed by a stone wall 1.5m thick and almost 2m high. The entrance was through a rectangular building that doubled as a gatehouse and barn. Within the spacious enclosure stood three more oblong buildings (used as stores and iron smelting workshops), while two round houses provided the domestic accommodation. Finds indicate that the settlement was occupied in the fourth century AD and must surely have been the seat of a local man of some standing. In the stony landscape of north Wales these farmsteads survive in great numbers and point to a well-established agricultural society, with enough surplus to invest in good houses. They are often labelled on maps as *Cytiau'r Gwyddelod* (Irishmen's huts) after a mistaken belief that they were built by Irish settlers in the Dark Ages. But perhaps the semi-fortified appearance of these settlements was prompted by the increasing threat of raids from across the sea, as the stability of the Roman Empire crumbled.

Plan and reconstruction drawings of enclosed farmsteads in north Wales:
Glasgoed (top)
and Hafoty-Ty-Newydd (bottom)

Places to visit

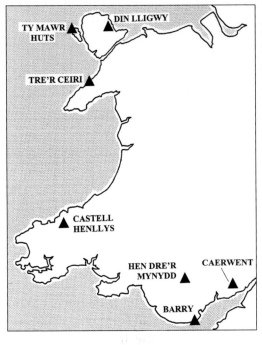

Barry *Cold Knap Roman building*

First discovered in 1960 and then fully excavated in 1980-81 in advance of redevelopment, this important Roman site was subsequently saved for posterity. Four wings of rooms connected by a veranda are ranged around a central courtyard, with a detached block (possibly a watchtower) at one corner. While the plan is typical of houses excavated across Wales, very little is known of its purpose. All the finds date from the mid-third to mid-fourth century AD, and the house's proximity to the site of a port suggests that it had a civil rather than domestic function. Perhaps it was a harbourmaster's residence or a guesthouse for maritime travellers. In the Dark Ages the crumbling building was briefly reoccupied and a small hut was built in the courtyard. (See plan and drawing p.19)

Access: Freely accessible. The site lies next to The Knap car park on the sea front, off the A4055 road from Barry town to Barry Island, Vale of Glamorgan (OS map ref: ST 099 664).

Blaenrhondda *Hen Dre'r Mynydd settlement*

On open moorland at the head of the Rhondda Valley lie the remains of the most substantial and accessible hut group in south Wales. Well-preserved drystone walls delineate a group of six enclosures with adjoining round houses, with outlying huts and pens scattered about the mountainside. The site was excavated in 1921 but insufficient dating material was found, although it is likely to be a native settlement of the late-Iron Age or Roman period.

Access: Freely accessible. The site lies next to a car park and picnic area on the A4061 mountain road from Treherbert to Hirwaun (OS ref: SN 923 019).

Caerwent *Venta Silurum Roman Town*

The excavated foundations at Caerwent offer the best opportunity to see the remains of Roman domestic buildings in Wales. Most surviving Roman remains in the country are forts and military bases, but Caerwent was a civil site, and was established late in the first century

AD to encourage the local tribes to come down from the hills. The first houses were built from timber, but over the years they were replaced with stone and brick. Along the principal street lay workshops, inns and shops, with houses and domestic buildings occupying the larger plots off the main centre. Around AD 330 the earthwork defences of the town were upgraded with stone walls and gateways, for the Empire was facing many external threats and throughout Roman Britain similar refortification was

Courtyard house at Pound Lane, Caerwent
(see also drawing and plan on pp. 17 and 19)

being carried out. Town life in Caerwent lingered on into the fifth century, but the evidence suggests that many buildings were empty and ruinous by then.

Now a busy road bypasses Caerwent and the little town is refreshingly free from urban over-development. The circuit of walls is largely intact and some of the internal buildings have been excavated and remain on display. Of particular relevance to this book are the three houses exposed in Pound Lane. Closest to the main road are two elongated 'strip houses' containing workshops at the front, with domestic accommodation at the rear. The remains of a drain and colonnade are clearly visible along the front. Behind this site are fragments of a larger house with suites of small rooms arranged around a central courtyard. Further along the lane can be seen the almost complete ground plan of an ambitious house with two internal courtyards. The southern part of the house had very plain rooms which may have been used as agricultural stores, but the main residential chambers were laid out around the smaller north courtyard. Here it is still possible to see the underfloor heating system that kept the winter chill away. The main rooms had mosaic floors and painted plaster walls, but only the bare stone foundations remain.

Access: The Roman remains are freely accessible at any reasonable time, and are located in Caerwent village, off the A48 Newport to Chepstow road, M48 junction 2 (OS map ref: ST 469 905).

Cardigan *Castell Henllys hillfort*

This is one of many Iron Age hillforts in Wales built and occupied during the period 600 BC to AD 100, but what makes this site unique is that some of the round houses have been reconstructed on their original foundations. Before work started, this settlement was no different from the countless neighbouring sites, overgrown with grass and bushes

Reconstructed Iron Age houses at Castell Henllys

and with no structures visible above ground apart from the earthworks massed on the only level approach to the fort. When the Romans conquered Wales the fort was abandoned and a new settlement was established later just outside the old defences.

Archaeologists have been excavating here since 1981, and work is still ongoing. The circular footings of numerous houses have been discovered and five have now been reconstructed using traditional materials and techniques. All were timber-framed with wattle and daub walls topped with a shaggy mop of thatch. The largest round house is known (with some justification) as the 'chieftain's house', for it measures 13m across and is almost 8m high inside. The roomy chamber has a central hearth surrounded by wooden benches and partitioned sleeping areas with woollen hangings give the place a homely feel. The whole arrangement is spacious, yet snug, and the smoke from the open fire is not too much of an ordeal for the eyes and nose. One reconstructed building has been interpreted as a grain store and has a raised wooden floor to keep the produce off the damp ground. Another is a smithy with a large hearth for iron working.

The reconstruction of these houses not only helps us to appreciate what Castell Henllys looked like over two thousand years ago, but also enables us to investigate the problems and solutions of early architecture. The natural resources needed to build one house indicate that the original occupants had to manage the local environment. Apart from the main supporting timbers, hundreds of hazel branches were needed for wattling, fifteen tons of clay for the daub walls and two thousand bundles of reeds for the roof.

The walls and timbers have been decorated with sinuous patterns favoured by the ancient Celts, as they may well have been originally – but such details would never be recovered by excavation alone and rely on imaginative interpretation of the end results.

Access: Castell Henllys is owned by the Pembrokeshire Coast National Park and is open daily 10-5 between Easter and October (phone 01239 891319 for details of events). The site lies 3km west of Eglwyswrw village, on the A487 from Cardigan to Fishguard road (OS map ref: SN 117 391).

Holyhead *Ty-mawr settlement*

Under the rugged peaks of Holyhead Mountain at this most distant tip of Wales, people have farmed the land for thousands of years. Some twenty stone-built structures and associated field enclosures can be seen along the gorse and bracken covered slopes, but many more once existed here. Although they look like typical Iron Age round houses, recent investigations have revealed that some were occupied as far back as the Neolithic. The whole settlement may in fact be a succession of farmsteads inhabited at various dates right up into the Dark Ages. Ten dwelling houses can be seen here, along with a similar number of smaller oval and rectangular structures (some partly cut into the ground), which were probably used as workshops or stores.

Access: In the care of CADW and freely accessible. Ty-mawr lies about 4km west of Holyhead, beside the road to South Stack (OS map ref: SH 211 820).

Llanaelhearn *Tre'r Ceiri hillfort*
One of the largest and most impressive Iron Age hillforts in Wales, Tre'r Ceiri ('the town of giants') crowns a rocky peak on the north coast of the Lleyn peninsula. Over 150 huts of round or oblong shape can be seen within the towering stone ramparts. (See photograph on p.13.) Finds from excavations indicate that the fort was occupied during Roman times, but it was probably built in at least two phases several centuries earlier. Like many such hillforts, it is difficult to say whether the site was permanently inhabited or only a temporary haven used during unsettled times. The large heap of stones on the summit is a Bronze Age burial mound.

Access: The village of Llanaelhearn lies on the A499 road between Caernarfon and Porthmadog. As you approach the village from the north, take the fork to Nefyn (B4417), and after 1.5km there is a small lay-by on the right. From here a footpath climbs steeply up the mountainside to the fort (OS map ref: SH 373 447).

Moelfre *Din Lligwy settlement*
Anglesey has a rich legacy of prehistoric sites and monuments; Neolithic burial chambers, Bronze Age standing stones and Iron Age settlements proliferate here. The island was the last stronghold of the Druids against the Roman invaders and the recovery of votive objects from the murky waters of Llyn Cerrig Bach reveals the wealth and influence of the Celtic ruling tribes. Long after the dust of battle had settled, a local chieftain established his HQ on a low cliff close to the

Reconstruction drawing of Din Lligwy

Remains of a round house at Din Lligwy

eastern edge of the island. Using great blocks of limestone hacked from the adjacent crags, the builders created a pentagonal-shaped courtyard containing three oblong and two round buildings. Another rectangular building doubled as a gatehouse and barn. All are now ruined and roofless, but we can envisage thatched roofs rising above the solidly built walls.

This is just one of hundreds of similar enclosed farmsteads found all over north Wales, but because it has been in State Guardianship since 1940 it is in an excellent state of preservation. During excavations pieces of imported pottery and glassware dating to the late-fourth century AD were found here, although it is likely that Din Lligwy had been occupied for many years before. The quality of the finds indicates that this was no squalid farm, but the high-status centre of a wealthy country estate.

Access: Din Lligwy is in the care of CADW and is freely accessible. It lies 2km west of Moelfre on Anglesey. From Menai Bridge follow the A5025 through Benllech and turn right towards Moelfre at the big roundabout, taking the first left down a narrow road. After passing a burial chamber you will find a small lay-by on the left, close to the ruins of a medieval chapel. Park here and walk across the fields to the site (OS map ref: SH 497 862).

Hut settlements in north-west Wales

Due to the predominately rocky landscape of north Wales, the native settlements in this region were built from stone and remain in a fair state of preservation. Hundreds of enclosed settlements and scattered hut sites are known, but very few have been excavated and so they could range in date from the late-Bronze Age to the end of the Roman period. The following is a selection of the more impressive and accessible sites; it is useful to consult the Caernarfonshire and Anglesey editions of the RCAHMW Inventories for additional information (see further reading list). Before setting out into the mountains it is advisable to get hold of detailed OS maps that will show most archaeological sites and public rights of way.

At **Hafod-y-gelyn** *(OS map ref: SH 676 716)* above Abergwyngregyn is an enclosed group of two huts on sloping ground. Several large boulders mark the entrance into the oval courtyard. The site can be found just uphill from a small parking area at the end of the road. From here an ancient trackway crosses Bwlch y Ddeufaen towards the village of Rowen, passing along the way a fine and varied collection of monuments (tombs, cairns, circles, standing stones, settlements). The track passes close to the prominent Neolithic burial chamber of Maen-y-bardd. Just past the stone tomb is an earthwork enclosure with two round huts inside *(SH 735 717)*; a single enclosed hut lies a little further along. The hillside around the chamber is covered with field enclosures and medieval house sites.

Several groups of huts are scattered along the Dwyfor and Glaslyn valleys in the foothills of Eryri. Most accessible is a group at **Cwm Dyli** *(SH 656 542)*, which can be reached by a footpath from Llyn Gwynant, or can be seen from a viewpoint on the A498 Capel Curig road. **Bryn y Castell** off the B4391 near Ffestiniog *(SH 728 429)* is a compact defended settlement on a rocky knoll, excavated and partly reconstructed in 1979-85. The site was occupied late in the Iron Age and was the scene of much industrial activity. After the Roman invasion the fort was abandoned, but in the second century another hut outside the defences was used for iron working. The rebuilt stone ramparts enclose a small oval courtyard and the positions of several round houses have been marked out in the grass.

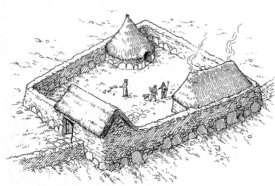

*Reconstruction drawing
of Hafoty Wernlas*

The fields surrounding Rhostryfan near Caernarfon are covered with extensive field systems and settlement sites, partly overlain by more modern walls and boundaries. The best site hereabouts is **Hafoty Wernlas** *(SH 501 583)*, which was excavated in 1921 and is reached along a footpath from the village. The stony foundations mark out a rectangular enclosure with round and oblong buildings inside; one was used as a gatehouse while the other contained two hearths and served as an iron-smelting workshop. Finds date the settlement to the late-Roman period. Close by is a much larger enclosure that may well have been the forerunner of the enclosed settlement.

A similar change of site seems to be represented by a scattering of farmsteads in the hills east of Llanaelhearn. The main stronghold is perched on top of Pen-y-gaer, while on the gentler slopes below are a handful of enclosed settlements presumably dating to the Roman period. The best examples are at **Llain-llan** (SH 408 449) and **Cwm Cilio** (SH 422 452). For the enthusiast, a particularly good group of huts and enclosures can be found high up on the slopes of **Graig Goch** near Dolbenmaen (SH 500 477), reached by a long walk from the A487. In sheltered hollows below the summit some thirty huts survive, their drystone construction and somewhat irregular shape bearing comparison with the more extensive Iron Age and Roman period settlement at Tre'r Ceiri not far away.

PART TWO
AD 500 - 1500

The Medieval Period

By the fourth century AD Rome had changed from being an empire on the offensive to one on the defensive. A sorry succession of short-lived rulers drained manpower and resources to bolster their own campaigns and the overstretched frontier was no longer an obstacle to the barbarian tribes searching for new lands to settle. In Britain, fortified bases were established along the southern coastline to deter the invaders, while the dwindling populations of towns and cities sought refuge behind defensive walls. All this had a devastating effect on the economy; trade declined, country estates were abandoned, and the import of overseas goods was interrupted. Even plague-carrying mosquitoes are blamed for contributing to the downfall of the Roman Empire. By the start of the fifth century only a shadow of Roman government remained in Britain after the army finally pulled out to deal with the worsening crises at home. In AD 410 the ineffectual Emperor Honorius turned his back on Britain, politely telling the civic authorities to look after their own defence.

Within a few generations, Saxon settlers from Europe had overrun a large portion of eastern Britain and pushed the native Romanised Celts into the far west and north of the country. What had been a relatively unified land now became fragmented into small kingdoms and petty realms, expanding and contracting with the ebb and flow of fortune, controlled by any dynasty ruthless enough to hold onto power. The only thing they had in common was the Christian faith, introduced in the latter days of the Roman Empire and bolstered by the efforts of hermits and holy men. This period (known by academics as 'Early Medieval' and everyone else as 'The Dark Ages') witnessed the emergence of a national identity as well as the rise of new Welsh leaders who struggled to bring some semblance of order to a country wracked by internal and external fighting.

The period between the fifth century and the Norman invasion at the end of the eleventh century can justly be termed the Dark Ages as far as the story of the Welsh house is concerned. Very little is known about the domestic life of the populace at this time, and even less about their homes. The archaeological record is slight, and a great deal of supposition is required to build up a picture. There is evidence to indicate that at first some old hillforts and hut sites were being reused, particularly by the new ruling classes. Deganwy, Dinorben and Dinas Emrys are pre-Roman fortified sites in north Wales that have produced domestic finds of Dark Age date, and tradition – coupled with literary sources in some cases – suggests that they were the courts of local bigwigs. Islands, caves and promontories were also utilised as settlement sites, evidently on the strength of their defensive capabilities.

What is certain is that at the end of the Roman period the building of round huts petered out and since then up to the present day virtually all houses have been constructed to an oblong plan with a ridged roofline. The advantage of a rectangular building is obvious: it can easily be divided up to form chambers of regular shape and, if more space is needed, it is a simple matter to add more rooms to one end, or build an adjoining wing. With a round house the basic shape cannot be extended or enlarged without weakening the structure.

Some information concerning the aristocratic houses of the time is provided by the Welsh Laws of King Hywel Dda (*c.*880-950), which were formulated in the tenth century but survive only in later manuscript versions. Peasants tied to the territory of a particular ruler were obliged to render services at certain times of the year and help with the construction and repair of the lordly *llys* (court). The buildings associated with this establishment would include a hall (*neuadd*), private chamber, kitchen, chapel, barn, stables and stores, with the poorer houses of the bondmen close by. A similar arrangement would have been found at the *maerdref* (the mayor, or reeve's township), which functioned as the administrative centre of the surrounding estate. The Laws even provide values for different parts of the buildings, almost like an insurance replacement cost in the event of a fire. The *neuadd* occupied an important place in medieval Welsh literature and society. This large multi-purpose chamber, warmed by a fire blazing on the floor, was filled with the noise, bustle and smells of daily life. The aristocratic halls would have provided accommodation for guests, travellers, bards and other courtly hangers-on, and the standing of a ruler would have been measured by his prowess in battle and his generosity towards his allies.

Archaeological investigations have uncovered a few of these early-medieval centres, of which the most notable stood at Dinas Powis near Cardiff. Here, within a lightly defended hilltop enclosure, lay two buildings of rectangular plan with rounded corners, the largest measuring internally about 13m by 5m and warmed by a hearth at one end of the chamber. Both buildings were marked by shallow ditches designed to draw away rainwater dripping from the thatched roofs – nothing else remained, for the walls were constructed from clay or stone and had long been robbed away. There were probably other buildings here as well, but the remains were too insubstantial to survive. A wide range of finds, including glassware, ceramic vessels and scrap metal, dated the occupation of the site to AD 400-600 and implied that the inhabitants had some trade links with Northern Europe and the Mediterranean.

More substantial remains of a lordly residence have been unearthed at **Llys Rhosyr** on Anglesey and the stone foundations have been preserved for public view. Although constructed at a much later date than Dinas Powis, this group of thirteenth-century buildings nevertheless gives an idea of the kind of dwellings occupied by the upper echelons of medieval Welsh society. The principal structure was a rather modest hall with timber-framed walls on stone footings. Three smaller stone buildings stood close by, one of them (perhaps a private chamber or parlour) being reached from the hall along a covered passageway. A rectilinear boundary wall enclosed the whole site.

By the tenth century, Anglo-Saxon settlers from England had pushed into native territory along the north coast of Wales and established the fortified borough of *Cledemutha* on the banks of the river Clwyd. The later town of Rhuddlan largely occupies the site, but archaeologists have found some post-holes and hollowed basements of vanished timber houses.

After the Saxons came the Vikings. From the ninth century onwards these Scandin-avian pirates raided the vulnerable coastal communities of Wales time after time, before settling down to establish more permanent habitations in Ireland, the Isle of Man and the Wirral district. Place-name evidence and artefacts have long pointed to a Viking presence on the island of Anglesey and explorations in a field near Llanbedrgoch in 1994 brought to light the remains of a permanent settlement of the period. Sometime between AD 450 and 850 there was a native settlement here comprising an archaic wattle round house and a rectangular timber hall sheltering within an earthwork bank and ditch. During the period 850–1000 the site was more strongly defended by a thick stone perimeter wall and the earlier structures were replaced by at least three timber-framed buildings. One was certainly a house, for it had a central hearth surrounded on three sides by low benches or sleeping platforms. The lower end of the building had a stone flagged floor and may have been used to pen cattle. The house measured 11.2m by 5.6m and was represented by some foundation stones, postholes and a sunken floor cut into the ground. Archaeologists from the National Museum of Wales believe this important site represents a farm, craft production centre and trading post rolled into one. A huge quantity of Viking-style artefacts was recovered from the excavations, pointing to some association with the Norsemen; but Llanbedrgoch could equally have been established as a native base, perhaps by King Rhodri Mawr (*c*.844-878) during his long and bloody campaign against the invaders.

Although the evidence for Dark Age domestic sites is so sparse, it is likely that most of the native population lived in dispersed farmsteads scattered about the land, a settlement pattern that largely endures to this day. There would have been the occasional cluster of houses around the territorial *llys*, but the familiar image of a rural village or town (complete with church, castle and manor house) was a concept introduced into Wales by another continental invader – the Normans. Like the Romans before them, the Normans found the conquest of Wales a much harder undertaking than the subjugation of Anglo-Saxon England. Shortly after arriving in Britain in 1066, the Normans looked west to the mountainous lands ruled by a plethora of petty kings and started two hundred-odd years

of struggle before the last native ruler was defeated. The invaders built hundreds of castles to consolidate their military achievements and fostered economic and spiritual growth through the establishment of new towns and religious centres.

The Normans seized most of the best agricultural land at an early date, parcelling it out amongst themselves and leaving the poorer uplands to the Welsh. It is in these bleak heights that

Remains of long huts at Nant Pennig in the Brecon Beacons

the greatest number of medieval houses can be found, because subsequent exploitation of the landscape has been minimal, resulting in less damage to the archaeological remains. These sites represent the flotsam and driftwood of human expansion at a time when the climate was marginally better than today, making these seemingly inhospitable wastes more amenable to pastoral life. The Archaeological Trusts of Wales have been compiling a database of deserted settlements in upland areas and the results have identified a number in excess of three thousand. Yet despite this proliferation, relatively few have been properly excavated and the scanty available evidence can only provide us with a broad overview as to their age and function.

All that can be seen of medieval peasant dwellings today are low mounds of earth and rubble, reinforced with boulder kerbs and drystone walls marking the outline of rectangular buildings. These are termed *long huts*. Some of the visible foundations would have supported vanished upper walls of clay or timber-framed construction, while others would have been wholly stone-built. The steeply pitched roofs were probably covered in moorland thatch or clods of turf. The cleric and chronicler Gerald of Wales (1146-1223) claimed that the Welsh did not build great stone palaces but contented themselves with 'wattled huts on the edges of the forest, put up with little labour or expense, but strong enough to last a year or so'. Gerald was a great raconteur and well known for exaggerating, but he may be describing the actual dwellings that the very poor of medieval Wales had to subsist in.

Long huts are sometimes found in association with round houses. This may be taken as evidence of a contemporary date, but more probably represents a tradition of farming in a particular area over a long period of time. A typical example of this grouping can be found at **Pen-y-gaer** in the Conwy valley. On the gentle slopes below an Iron Age hillfort the moorland is criss-crossed with a network of old field walls and enclosures, interspersed with ruined cottages and the boulder foundations of several long huts. Three houses at

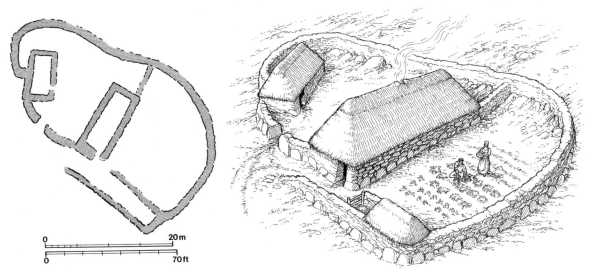

Plan and reconstruction of a long hut settlement at Maen-y-bardd (Rowen)

33

the eastern edge of the site adjoin a circular enclosure, which could have been an outlying dwelling of the fort reused as a stock pen.

In many upland areas the steep slopes made it necessary for houses to be constructed on artificial terraces. The builders would dig into the hillside and heap the spoil on the slope in front, creating a level rectangular platform on which to raise a house. Although such insubstantial dwellings have decayed away over the centuries, the platforms they stood upon remain to mark their former existence. These so-called *house platforms* were first recognised as a distinctive archaeological feature in the 1930s when excavations took place at several sites on **Gelligaer Common** near Merthyr Tydfil. The investigations revealed traces of crude buildings with turf and rubble walls and a low roof propped up by a row of central posts. The few datable finds suggest that at least one of the Gelligaer sites was inhabited during the late thirteenth and early fourteenth centuries. The prominent downhill alignment of the platform building was a sensible arrangement in a damp upland landscape, since only the narrowest end of the house faced any surface water draining down the slope. Some of the platforms even had banks curving around the scooped-out upper end to divert excess water. It was probably this need for adequate drainage that led to a marked preference for the downhill siting of farm buildings in succeeding centuries.

In 1961 another group of house platforms and enclosures was investigated at Beilibedw near Rhayader and here the dating evidence suggested occupation in the fifteenth and sixteenth centuries. The excavators found no sign of internal postholes and since the walls were too flimsy to bear any weight, the roofs must have been carried on self-supporting paired trusses (known as crucks) rising from the ground to the apex of the roof. More recently, excavations have been carried out on a group of platforms at Gesail Gyfarch near Porthmadog, onetime seat of the Welsh lords of Penyfed, and burned to the ground by Owain Glyndŵr as punishment for their English leanings. Rather surprisingly, given the high status of the site, the excavators found little evidence of a major structural building here, and the sparse finds pointed to a broad period of occupation between the thirteenth and sixteenth centuries.

Since long huts and house platforms are often found in pairs or small groups, they could represent single farmsteads with multiple buildings for different uses. This is likely to be the case with the Gelligaer sites, for the excavators did not always find convincing evidence of domestic occupation within the buildings. In 1977 archaeologists investigated a settlement at Cefn Graianog near Porthmadog and discovered the stone foundations of four timber-framed buildings set side-by-side. One was clearly a house (for it had a central hearth on the clay floor) while the others were interpreted as a cowshed, stable and barn. Finds pointed to occupation in the twelfth and thirteenth centuries. More recent excavations of long huts at Hafod Rhug Uchaf near Caernarfon, and Tro'r Derlwyn near Brynaman, indicated an eighteenth-century date.

Clearly platforms and long huts have a broad date range and a superficial examination will not always provide a clue to age. Nor is it possible to say without detailed excavation whether a long hut was wholly domestic or sheltered people and their livestock. Such dual-purpose dwellings resonate through the history of native domestic architecture and are now known by a descriptive term coined by Iorwerth Peate out of the old Welsh word *ty hir* – the long-house.

In Europe the origin of shared dwellings goes back to prehistoric times, but the long-house appears to have spread to Britain along with Scandinavian settlers in the ninth and tenth centuries AD and proliferated during the Middle Ages. Probably the earliest and certainly the most oft-quoted description of such a building appears in the collection of medieval Welsh folk-tales *The Mabinogion*:

> They saw an old hall, very black and having an upright gable whence issued a great smoke; and on entering they found the floor full of puddles and mounds, and it was difficult to stand thereon, so slippery was it with the mire of cattle … and there were boughs of holly spread over the floor, whereof the cattle had browsed the sprigs … Being weary they sought to sleep, but when they looked at the raised platform there was on it only a little short straw full of dust and fleas.

The unknown author of this extract from *The Dream of Rhonabwy* may be exaggerating the poverty of this particular hall, but the description cannot be far from the reality of life in a dual-purpose dwelling.

Some authorities believe that the appearance of the long-house was due to a deterioration of the climate in the fourteenth century, at a time when the peasant economy was undergoing economic growth. Cattle had to be wintered indoors to protect them from the weather and prevent the summer pastures from being trampled. By joining the cowshed to the house, the farmer could keep a close eye on his valuable livestock and benefit from the additional body heat to warm the chilly dwelling. Such practical considerations became enmeshed in the realms of folklore, for in parts of the country it was believed that cows would produce more milk if they could see the fire and that the warm glow would frighten away harmful spirits. Whatever the reasons behind the adoption of this archaic type of dwelling, long-houses had a lengthy lifespan in the remoter uplands of western Britain. An account written as late as 1916 describes a Denbighshire hill farm as 'a single long building, the animals and those who cared for them living together, a place so similar to Noah's Ark as can be imagined'.

A long hut at Cwm twrch (Brynaman)

Another aspect of bygone pastoral life that long huts must represent is the ancient practice of seasonal migration, known as *transhumance*. Farmers would take their cattle to graze in the high pastures for the summer months, leaving behind their permanent homesteads (the *hendre*) and residing for a time in an upland *hafod* ('summer house') or *lluest* ('encampment'). The scarcity of domestic debris found at some excavated long huts could be explained by such temporary occupation. Ordnance Survey maps reveal a plethora of *hafod* place-names across the country, showing how widespread the concept of this practice was, even though in reality it seems unlikely that every farming community migrated *en masse* to the hills for a summer break. Documentary evidence relating to *hafotai* goes back at least to the thirteenth century. In a survey of the estates seized by King Edward I from the Welsh princes many such sites are listed, including a settlement at '*Crombroinok*' that can still be identified today as a group of stone huts at **Cwm Brwynog** on the slopes of Eryri.

By Tudor times the growth of sheep farming and the enclosure of mountain pasturelands caused a decline in summer migrations, yet the *hafod* tradition lingered on in parts of the north well into the nineteenth century. The most famous description of Welsh *hafotai* was provided by Thomas Pennant in his book *A Tour in Wales* (1778-1783):

> These houses consist of a long low room, with a hole at one end to let out the smoke from the fire which is made beneath. Their furniture is very simple, stones are the substitute of stools, and the beds are of hay ranged along the sides … During the summer the men pass the time either in harvest work or in tending the herds; the women in milking or making butter and cheese … The diet of these mountaineers is very plain, and consists of butter-cheese and oat bread or Bara Ceirch … Towards winter they descend to the *Hen Dref* or old dwelling.

Although Pennant was writing at the end of the eighteenth century, his description of the lifestyle and homes of the *hafod* farmer cannot have been very different from the domestic world of the medieval peasant.

This is not to say that home comforts were vastly better for the conquerors. There was little structural difference between an upland long hut and a poorer dwelling in one of the new settlements springing up in the wake of the Norman invasion. Many of these urban endeavours thrived, expanded and remain with us today, such as Cardiff, Chepstow, Monmouth, Pembroke and Tenby. Some were not so fortunate; once their bustling heyday was over they dwindled away to just a few houses, or failed altogether. Such was the fate of **Runston** near Chepstow. This deserted village lies on a breezy hilltop overlooking the Severn estuary and is dominated by the stark shell of a twelfth-century church. A muddy lane is all that is left of the village street, flanked by low mounds and hollows marking the remains of at least twenty houses.

When archaeologists began excavating at **Cosmeston** near Cardiff in the 1980s, only vague earthworks remained of this fourteenth-century hamlet, but after exposing the stone foundations it was decided to rebuild the houses and preserve the site as a sort of

A reconstructed medieval house at Cosmeston near Cardiff

'living museum'. The village grew up beside a manor house established here by the Constantines, one of many Norman families who settled in the fertile Vale of Glamorgan during the twelfth century. The Black Death struck and wounded this little village, but did not finish it off, and the settlement lingered on for many years until in the nineteenth century just one cottage was left standing. Four medieval houses have now been reconstructed. Their interior layouts are broadly the same: a single rectangular room with an open hearth at one end, around which the family sat, cooked and ate. Furniture was sparse and very basic, just a few wooden benches and stools, with manger-like beds against the side walls. Everything above foundation level has been rebuilt using traditional methods and the end result gives a vivid impression of the standard of living an average medieval person might expect.

Surviving Medieval Houses

As previously mentioned, Welsh houses built before 1400 mainly endure as ruined walls, excavated foundations or very rare fragments embedded in later structures. The paucity of intact buildings must be largely due to the long years of warfare between the Welsh and the English. The last great outbreak of violence was the revolt of Owain Glyndŵr, which lasted from 1400 to about 1412. Owain's attempt to break from the English Crown and rule unchallenged over Welsh Wales led to scorched-earth tactics and reprisals against anyone supporting the wrong side. The devastation caused by the uprising depleted the ancient timber halls of the gentry and only after the English forces regained control of the country could rebuilding occur.

Until recently, the dating of early houses was a largely conjectural process based on comparisons with buildings over the border in England, for the useful practice of inscribing a date was only taken up with enthusiasm in the late sixteenth century. Fortunately, the RCAHMW has recently carried out a project to date various timber buildings in Wales by a method known as dendrochronology, using the annual growth rings of a tree to calculate a felling date. Every year a tree forms a growth ring beneath the bark and this process is affected by climatic conditions (a good growth year will produce a thick ring, while a bad season leaves a thin one). By comparing a sample cut from ancient timbers with an established regional pattern of rings from a living tree, it is possible to pinpoint the exact year a particular tree was felled.

The evidence so far gathered by this method indicates that many of our surviving halls belong to a rebuilding phase in the late fifteenth and early sixteenth century; in fact, until a few years ago the earliest date obtained was 1417-20 for **Aberconwy House**. Then in 2004 an ornate roof truss embedded within the later masonry walls of Hafod-y-Garreg Farm, near Erwood, was tested and produced a rather surprising felling date. The evidence unequivocally pointed to the oak frame having been cut and assembled in the summer of 1402, at a time when the Glyndŵr rebellion was in full swing. Only this single truss survived the subsequent rebuilding, but Hafod-y-Garreg is currently reckoned to be the oldest standing house in Wales. Its survival is almost miraculous, and the fact that the house was built at all during such a troubled period of Welsh history suggests that the owner was either oblivious to the events taking place around him, or very optimistic about the future.

Techniques and materials

For the craftsmen who created these houses there were principally only two building materials to use – stone and wood – and these had to be obtained from the immediate locality. All except the very wealthy used what was to hand, and the distribution of stone and timber buildings across the country is therefore dependant upon what was available locally. The bedrock of Wales had provided abundant building supplies from earliest times; walls were constructed from rubble with carefully shaped blocks for the corners, doors and window frames. Those with enough money built their house entirely from dressed stone, or at least used stone to provide an attractive facing to the façade most people would see. Thin slabs of stone or slate would be used for roof coverings. Timber was used extensively for major structural supports such as roof trusses and floor beams, and also for lintels, doors and window frames.

Some houses had their walls built from clay, an ancient form of construction still used in many parts of the world today and known in Wales as clom or cob. The process involved mixing clay with straw or animal hair to act as a binding agent, then building the walls up in layers to the requisite height. A coat of limewash helped protect the exterior against the effects of the weather. This simple material was generally reserved for the dwellings of the poorest members of society, but recent investigations at **Hafoty** on Anglesey suggest that it was also utilised for some upper class homes. Because of their perishable nature surviving clay-walled cottages tend to be relatively recent in date, although they represent a building tradition stretching back many centuries.

The close relative of mud is brick. The Romans introduced this now-familiar material into Britain, but with the collapse of the Empire the manufacturing process fell into abeyance for centuries. In Wales building bricks re-appeared in the sixteenth century, but it was not until the growth of the railway network in the Victorian era that the material achieved its almost universal popularity.

Despite the predominately stony nature of the Welsh landscape, the majority of early houses were almost wholly constructed from wood. They are known as 'half-timbered' or more correctly, timber-framed buildings and were once common throughout Wales except in the far north and south-west. Towns such as Caernarfon, Cardiff, Conwy and Machynlleth were originally timber-framed; but so great has been the subsequent rebuilding in stone and brick that the present distribution of timber houses has shrunk to a broad band extending along the eastern edge of the country bordering England. Here in the Welsh Marches will be found some of the finest surviving examples of timber-framed buildings in Britain.

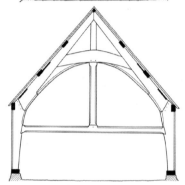
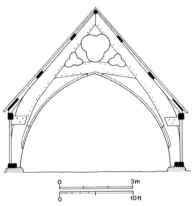

Examples of cruck frames.
Top: Base cruck at Bryndethol, Llangollen.
Middle: Jointed cruck, Pant Glas, Denbigh.
Bottom: Ornate cruck with cusping, Middle Maestorglwydd, Hay

Timber-framed houses

Aside from the materials used, there are fundamental differences between stone and timber-framed buildings. Stone houses were built *in situ*; sturdy trusses resting on the wall tops transferred the downward thrust of the heavy roof through the solid masonry to the ground. Timber-framed buildings were constructed from a skeletal framework of posts, rather than load-bearing walls, supporting the structural integrity, and they were prefabricated at a carpenter's yard and then reassembled at a designated plot. The esoteric symbols and marks often visible on beams are assembly aids to help the builder to put the structure together correctly.

There were two ways the medieval carpenter could make this framework, by using either **cruck trusses** or **box-frames**. Crucks are self-supporting frames ideally suited to the open halls of the medieval period. Each cruck truss was shaped out of the trunk and main branch of a mature oak tree, then split down the middle to create a pair of mirror-image timbers with a characteristic curved profile. The paired timbers were pegged together to form a truss shaped like a capital A, sweeping up from the ground to the apex of the roof, and the truss was set upright on a stone foundation plinth to prevent the damp ground from rotting the wood. This is the classic and most commonly encountered form of cruck-truss, but there also exist several variations on this theme. Some crucks were assembled from shorter pieces of timber and only rise as high as the collar (the horizontal reinforcing strut of an A-frame); these are termed **base-**

crucks. An even simpler version, known as a ***scarfed-cruck***, is made up of overlapping lengths of timber pegged together at the 'bend' or elbow. These crude trusses are commonly found in the mud-built cottages of west Wales, since the walls are incapable of supporting much weight and the impoverished occupants would not have been overly concerned with fine carpentry.

Crucks were widely used in medieval halls between the twelfth and sixteenth centuries and survive in great numbers in the Welsh Marches and western parts of England. However, when houses on two or more floors gained in popularity, crucks rapidly fell out of favour because the curved shape of the blades restricted headroom in the upper part of the building. To solve this problem, trusses were sometimes raised part way up the wall, creating ***raised-crucks***. Nevertheless, the cruck tradition did not wholly die out and many seventeenth-century houses have roof trusses with prominent curved feet, termed ***upper-crucks***.

The other framing method used by the medieval carpenter was the ***box-frame***. This proved more adaptable since it could be assembled from shorter pieces of wood and offered greater headroom. A box-frame consists of two separate elements – the A-frame roof truss and the wall-posts it sits on. Generally the roof truss is fixed into a large horizontal beam (known as a tie-beam), which spans the width of the building at eaves height. From the mid sixteenth century onwards most timber houses were built in this way, although a few display a curious mix of the two types of framing, the ornate cruck usually being reserved for the central space of the hall.

Whatever the method of framing used, additional timbers were used to divide up the walls and internal partitions into variously sized rectangular panels; the panels were then infilled with wattle and daub. This involved fixing upright staves into the open panel and then weaving thin hazel branches between the staves to create

Exposed cruck in a derelict cottage near Wrexham

Jointed cruck at Pant Glas, Denbigh

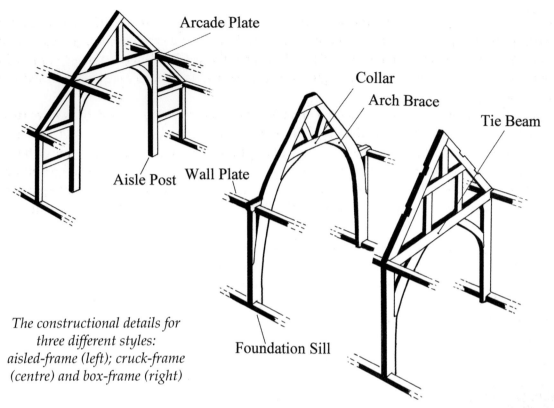

Arcade Plate

Collar

Arch Brace

Tie Beam

Aisle Post   Wall Plate

Foundation Sill

The constructional details for three different styles: aisled-frame (left); cruck-frame (centre) and box-frame (right)

wattling. Over this would be smeared a mix of clay, lime, dung and straw (or horse hair), which dried to a hard shell and was then given a protective coat of limewash. Wattle and daub structures had been used to make houses as far back as the Iron Age, as we have seen, but the timber-framed buildings of the later Middle Ages are a far cry from the crude homes of the Celts. Indeed, they have been ranked among the most beautiful buildings ever made. Anyone who has visited the towns of Chester, Leominster, Ludlow or Shrewsbury will be able to appreciate the carpentry skills needed to create the complex framework and decorative panels.

While many people will be familiar with 'black and white' houses and their innumerable modern copies, it is important

An impressive box-frame truss at Neuadd Cynhinfa (Dolanog). Note the smoke blackened timbers, a sure sign of a former open hall

to realise that this starkly contrasting scheme is due to Victorian tastes. Originally the buildings would have been completely limewashed, or the daub panels given an ochre wash and the woodwork left to age into a subtle silvery grey. Wattle and daub requires frequent maintenance and decaying panels were often replaced with cheaper alternatives (such as brick) in subsequent years. The commonplace thatched roof ultimately suffered a similar fate, ousted in favour of the more durable and readily available slate.

An example of box-frame construction at Tretower Court, near Crickhowell

Towards the end of the Middle Ages an ancient form of roof structure made a re-appearance in mid and north Wales. ***Aisled-frames*** had been in use during Roman and Saxon times to solve the problem of roofing wide buildings. Because timber trusses can only span a certain distance, builders relied on a line of internal pillars to carry the weight of an extended roof. These pillars (more properly known as arcade posts) effectively divided the hall into three areas – a central nave, and two narrower side aisles, much as you would see in a large church or cathedral. The posts hold up horizontal beams (arcade plates) running the length of the building, on which the lesser roof timbers rest. Aisled construction is quite common in England and was used for ecclesiastical, domestic and agricultural buildings, but in Wales there are far fewer examples. Only one fully aisled building has been recorded, but there are a further nineteen examples of partially

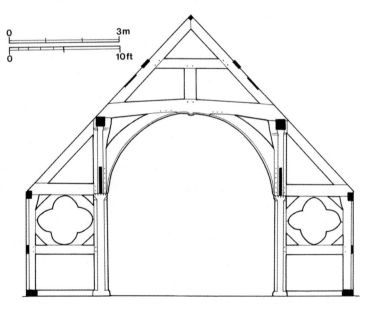

An example of aisled-frame construction at Ty Mawr, Castle Caereinion

aisled houses. The best and most complete example is the recently restored **Ty Mawr** (Castle Caereinion), which was built around 1460. All the internal partition walls are aisled box-frames, but the hall itself is spanned by a huge base-cruck (see photograph on p.xi). At the lower end of the hall there is an additional aisled frame, termed a *spere-truss*. Houses such as **Penarth Fawr** (Pwllheli) only have a spere-truss, which seems to have been intended primarily to create an impressive and ornamental approach to the hall.

The natural successor to the aisled frame was a *hammer-beam* roof. This type of roof structure consists of a horizontal cantilevered beam projecting from the wall top and supporting the base of the truss. This clever device made it possible to built wide halls without the need for intrusive pillars. The greatest of all hammer-beam roofs can be seen at Westminster Hall in London, built in the 1390s to replace an older aisled structure. A forest of exquisitely carved beams supports an enormous roof span of 21 metres. By the end of the fifteenth century the ornate glories of hammer-beam roofs were appearing in the churches and great houses of north Wales. The finest example is Cochwillan (Bangor) built by William ap Gruffudd, a fervent supporter of the new Tudor dynasty. Just as the spere-truss is a decorative derivative of a functional aisled frame, so in Wales the hammer-beam is more for show than support. Effect is what the owners of these grand halls looked for and the hammer-beam roof lasted well beyond the medieval period – the last dated example having been built in 1626 at Coed-y-cra (Northop).

Form and layout
At all levels of medieval society the concept of a house was based on one large room – the hall – where all domestic and social activity took place. In its simplest form the hall was a single room heated by a hearth burning on the floor, just like the peasant long huts previously described. Timber-framed or wattle screens might have partitioned the interior, creating divisions between the various functions of the communal room. From such humble beginnings the grandest of medieval houses developed. The internal layout of the hall developed into a fairly rigid plan that reflected the contemporary social structure – important people at the top, less important at the bottom. The most commonly adopted plan was a central hall with a set of rooms at either end, usually on two floors (*Figure A,* overleaf).

A typical example which can be explored in detail is Middle Maestorglwydd. This lies in the hills close to Hay-on-Wye and is a fifteenth-century cruck-framed hall. It has not been tested by dendrochronology, but comparison with other buildings would suggest that it was built around the middle of the century. The walls may have been timber-framed originally, but they were soon rebuilt in more durable masonry; otherwise the house is remarkably little altered, for it declined in status and was used as a barn from an early date, so escaping further modifications.

The arched entrance was in the long side of the house and opened onto a cross-passage leading through to another doorway in the opposite wall. On one side of the passage a timber-framed partition divided off the service rooms (basic chambers used for storing provisions). These are also termed *outer rooms* since they occupy the 'outside' or entry side of the hall, at its socially lower end. The most common arrangement was to have a pair of doors in the passage-partition leading to the pantry (a food store) and buttery (where drinks were kept). Some houses have three doors, the extra door opening onto a stairway to the upper chamber, or else leading through to an outside kitchen. External kitchens and bakeries were quite common in the medieval period to reduce the risk of a fire. At Maestorglwydd there is an unusually wide single doorway in the service partition, which seems to imply that this end of the building was used as a cowshed or stable. The chamber above the service room would have been used for storage or servants' sleeping accommodation, and was reached by a ladder-stair from the cross passage. These 'inferior' service rooms are mirrored by a suite of 'superior' chambers at the

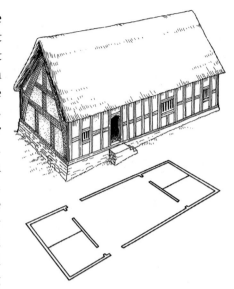

Figure A: a house comprising a central hall flanked by rooms

other end of the hall; these are termed the *inner rooms* and they generally contained a parlour and private sleeping chamber for the owner and his immediate family.

Between the two sets of rooms lay the great space of the hall itself, warmed by an open fire burning on the floor. The thick smoke drifted up into the lofty roof space and escaped through a vent or seeped through the thatched covering. This was the only fire in the house and it was used for cooking as well as for keeping warm. The central truss spanning the hall was elaborately decorated with cusping and windbraces, all now blackened after years of smoke from the hearth. The central truss of an open hall often ranks as the finest work produced by the medieval carpenter, but it is perhaps doubtful whether their skill was ever fully appreciated in the sooty gloom. The only light to glimmer inside would have come from candles or rush lamps, or what daylight filtered through the open doors and windows. Glass was such an expensive commodity that only the higher echelons of society could afford it, so most windows were just holes in the walls filled with stout wooden bars for security and shuttered against the wind. Because the windows were positioned on either side of the house, the shutters could be opened on the flank sheltered from the prevailing breeze. One of these little wooden window frames still survives at Maestorglwydd.

Within this dark, draughty, smoky barn of a building, the proud owner and his family would sit at the high table presiding over the guests and servants. The table was placed at the upper end of the hall to impress upon anyone entering the house just who was boss. It might also be set on a raised platform (a dais) to further emphasise the importance of the owner. At Maestorglwydd there was a shallow recess in the partition wall for a bench, so that those sitting at the table would be protected from soot falling on their heads. In some

*A cutaway drawing of Middle Maestorglwydd showing a central hall
with service rooms to the right of the entrance, and the private chambers beyond the high table*

grand halls this simple feature was enlarged as a decorated canopy extending over the dais. Beyond the high table another timber-framed partition divided off the private inner rooms.

Making the dais partition gave the carpenter a further opportunity to display his skills. In many houses this took the form of a post-and-panel screen formed of interlocking upright oak panels. A particularly monumental example can be seen at **Tretower Court** (see overleaf). Despite the obvious expense of producing such fine pieces of carpentry, the owners of Neuadd Cynhinfa (Dolanog) opted to have *all* their walls (inside and out) built in this fashion. Evidently they had a great love of wood panelling! The hall was built in 1507 on a hilltop overlooking the Banwy valley and underwent considerable alterations in 1630 when a stone fireplace and upper floor were inserted. Although most of the timber walls were later rebuilt in stone, enough details survive to make a partial reconstruction possible and some of the decorative framework has been exposed by recent renovation work. Long after the medieval period ended, the post-and-panel partition remained in favour and added grace and grandeur to even the smallest house.

The threefold division of the medieval house (outer rooms / hall / inner rooms) fulfilled a hierarchical role and emphasised the social standing of the owners. It endured well beyond the medieval period, as we shall see in the next section. This basic tripartite layout was subject to minor variations. The inner room end of the house might be built as a cross-wing (*Figure B*), as can be seen at Llwyncelyn (Cwmyoy), Glebe Farm (Gower), and **Hafoty** for instance. The early sixteenth-

The partition screen at Tretower Court

century cruck hall at Cefn Ceido (Rhayader) has a cross-wing at the passage end of the house; another unusual feature here is the window at first-floor level looking into the hall, allowing anyone in the upper chamber to keep a watchful eye on events below. In the later Middle Ages a particularly popular design was to have cross-wings at *both* ends of the hall, resulting in an ambitious H-plan house (*Figure C*) such as Penarth (Newtown) (see photo p.*viii*), Plasnewydd (Ruabon), and **Hafoty** (in its final form).

Although the vast majority of halls at this time were heated by open hearths, houses with stone walls were sometimes provided with integral fireplaces and chimneys. **Llys Euryn,** Colwyn Bay, **Tretower Court,** and Cochwillan are large houses with original fireplaces in

Llwyncelyn, Cwmyoy, a hall-house with a parlour cross-wing at the upper end

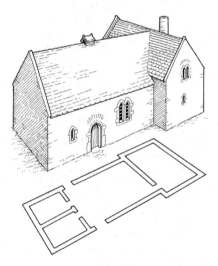

Figure B: a house with a single cross-wing

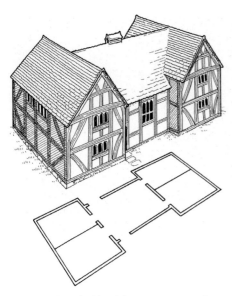

Figure C: a hall with two cross-wings

the halls and private rooms. The preference for private rooms rather than the more public hall started quite early on. The fourteenth-century poet William Langland wrote: 'Now have the rich a rule to eat by themselves in a privy parlour … or in a chamber with a chimney, and leave the chief hall that was made for meals, for men to eat in'. But it was not until the early years of the sixteenth century that the fireplace began to appear in greater numbers, heralding a radical change in the design and layout of the home.

All the buildings described above are classed as *hall-houses*, because they consist primarily of a ground-floor hall open to the roof. But there exists another important branch of medieval domestic architecture in which the principal chamber lies on an upper floor above secondary rooms or stores – the *first-floor hall*. This type of dwelling probably derives its ancestry from the castles and fortified houses of the upper classes, where security dictated the need for high-level living. Castles are outside the scope of this book, but it is important to bear in mind that at the heart of each glowering fortress was a domestic hall, just like any other. Pembrokeshire has the largest number of first-floor halls in Wales. They are all stone built, due to the lack of good timber and the absence of traditional carpentry skills, and the upper hall is invariably supported on vaulted undercrofts. As far back as 1603 the historian George Owen could write that 'most castles and houses of any account were built with vaults very strongly and substantially wrought', and it is this inherent strength that has ensured their survival to this day.

Another distinctive feature to have found its way down from the castle into domestic architecture at an early date in Pembrokeshire is the enclosed fireplace and chimney. Characteristic round stacks are dotted all over the area, particularly in the vicinity of Tenby, St Davids and Pembroke. Some are so massive that they have outlasted the house they were built for! They are usually called 'Flemish chimneys' after the Flemish immigrants who settled in this part of Wales in the twelfth century, but there is no historical evidence for this connection. In the countryside around St Davids there existed a fascinating group of buildings that apparently developed from the hall-house rather than the first-floor variety. These buildings were characterised by huge conical chimneys and small recesses (*outshuts*) projecting out from the side walls. Outshuts have also been recorded in Gower and both areas had strong ties with the West Country, where similar houses can still be seen. Unfortunately, the St Davids buildings have been altered out of all recognition since they were first recorded in the early years of the twentieth century and the best surviving example of this type is Garn near Fishguard, which still retains most of the features associated with this rare group.

Many more first-floor halls remain in Pembrokeshire, though they have undergone considerable alterations or have been left to fall into ruin. They range in size from diminutive single-roomed buildings like **Carswell** (St Florence), to larger upper-class residences at Flimston, Lydstep and Scotsborough (Tenby). Crowning them all are the monumental Episcopal palaces at **Lamphey** and **St Davids**. Some of these first-floor halls show signs of defensive capabilities and bridge the gap between the purely domestic

House at St Florence showing a typical Pembrokeshire 'Flemish chimney'

dwelling and the military castle tower. The upper chamber at **Carswell** was accessed by a ladder that could be drawn up inside in the event of an attack, while the much more ambitious Eastington (Rhoscrowther) had wall-walks and battlements. This seems to have been the defended cross-wing of an undefended ground-floor hall.

The desire for defence at the cost of domestic comfort was taken to its extreme with the *tower-house*. Wales has several examples including **Candleston** (Bridgend), **Ty Gwyn** (Barmouth) and **Gwydyr Castle** (Llanrwst), but nowhere near the huge numbers surviving in northern England, Scotland and Ireland (and this may be taken as an indication of the relative peace and stability of the Tudor countryside here). The finest of all the Welsh tower-houses is the **Old Rectory** at Angle, a fifteenth-century high-rise refuge for the lords of the manor (see photograph opposite). Inside, there is a vaulted ground floor store and three upper living rooms barely 4m square, linked by a cramped stair spiralling up to the battlements. Long after there was a need for defence, architectural features inspired by the castle continued to appear in upper class houses. Towers, mock battlements and gatehouses found favour with the rich and their imitators – all designed to show off and impress visitors, rather than to keep hordes of rebellious Welshmen at bay.

Places to visit

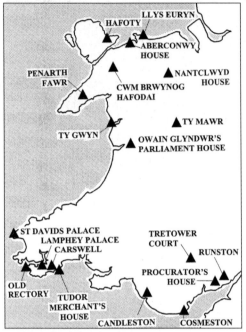

Angle *The Old Rectory*

The so-called Old Rectory at Angle is arguably the finest example of a tower-house surviving in Wales. This architectural crossbreed between a castle and a house is more commonly found in Scotland and the Scottish borders, where for centuries the lawless conditions made defence a necessity. The Old Rectory was probably built by the Shirburn family around 1400 to improve the defences of their coastal manor house in this exposed part of the peninsula.

Documentary sources indicate that there were other buildings here, but only the tower and part of the surrounding moat survive today. The only access into the tower was a doorway at first-floor level, protected by a drawbridge and some kind of porch. Inside there are three small chambers stacked on top of a vaulted storeroom, with a stair turret rising to the roof. Although the battlements have fallen, the row of large stone brackets that once supported them can still be seen. Such a building could never have withstood a prolonged siege by a sizeable army, but against a gang of thieves or pirates it would have proved very effective. In the event of an attack the lords of the manor could beat a hasty retreat inside, pull up the drawbridge, bar the door and wait things out; or else clamber up to the battlements and throw stones on their unwelcome visitors.

Access: The tower is in the care of the Pembrokeshire Coast National Park and is usually open daily in the summer months. At other times the key may be available from the adjacent house. It lies north of Angle village, 13km west of Pembroke on the B4320 signposted to Castlemartin (OS map ref: SM 866 030).

The Old Rectory, Angle

Barmouth *Ty Gwyn*

According to tradition Gruffydd Fychan built Ty Gwyn in the 1460s as a stronghouse and refuge for his Lancastrian allies during the Wars of the Roses. This dual purpose may explain some unusual features of the building and why it is not well planned for domestic comfort. Each floor contains one long and narrow room with tiny windows and a single fireplace inconveniently located in the gable wall (the opposite end must have been rather chilly). The large fireplace on the ground floor is built into the natural bedrock.

The main upper chamber, with its elaborate roof of seven oak trusses, now contains an exhibition about the Tudor dynasty and the maritime history of Barmouth. Several old photographs on display show Ty Gwyn before modern restoration work; the alterations carried out over the years had so thoroughly disguised the building that for a long time it was thought to have been destroyed. Gruffudd's home is commemorated in a poem by the bard Tudur Penllyn who described it as 'a house half in the waves … lofts higher than the mountains of Anglesey' and compared the strength of its walls to Caernarfon Castle! Needless to say, any bard of the time wishing to earn his place at the lord's table would be expected to pen such flattering phrases.

Access: The museum on the first floor is open daily during the summer months, while the ground floor is now used as a restaurant. Ty Gwyn stands next to the harbour in Barmouth, on the Mawddach estuary between Harlech and Dolgellau (OS map ref: SH 614 154).

Bridgend *Candleston Castle*

This is not a true castle but a defended manor of the Cantilupe family, now ruined and half-buried in the creeping sands of the Merthyr Mawr warren. It was built in the first half of the fourteenth century and underwent many alterations before being abandoned around 1900. The original domestic wing lay at the north end of an enclosed courtyard and to this was added a square tower that doubled as a private chamber and keep. The ground floor contains a dark vaulted storeroom, while the first floor is a single livingroom with doors leading to a privy and stair. Thus Candleston resembles the hall/tower combinations often found in south Pembrokeshire.

Access: Candleston Castle is privately owned, but there is public access to some parts of the building. It lies about 5km south-west of Bridgend and can be reached by following the signs to Merthyr Mawr. Pass through the village and the castle will be found beside the car park at the end of the road (OS map ref: SS 872 773).

Castle Caereinion *Ty Mawr*

When this important medieval house was discovered in 1971 it was disguised as a tumbledown barn with crumbling brick walls and a corrugated metal roof. Now, after years of careful and sympathetic restoration, the transformation is complete, making this architectural gem one of the finest medieval houses surviving in Wales. Ty Mawr is particularly important because it is one of only a handful of aisled halls in the country. The

Reconstruction drawing of the central hall at Ty Mawr, Castle Caereinion

building is almost 8m wide, and the only way the carpenters could create such a span was by using aisle posts. These posts support a horizontal beam (known as an arcade plate) running parallel to the sides of the building some distance above the ground, on which the roof timbers rest. The most obvious element of the aisled construction is the decorative spere truss, enriched with chamfered posts and quatrefoil panels, which served to divide off the cross-passage from the hall. Within the great space of the hall an enormous base-cruck sweeps up in a graceful curve to the arcade-plate.

Archaeological investigations have proved that Ty Mawr was built from timber felled in 1458-60 and that there was an earlier building on the same site. The size and quality of the house prove that someone of high social standing built it; yet despite its status Ty Mawr was a long-house, and the outer room at the lower end of the hall was used as a cowshed. Around 1594 the owners increased the accommodation by inserting an upper floor into the roofspace above the inner room. Then in 1631 a timber-framed chimney with back-to-back fireplaces was built to replace the original central hearth. From then on the story is one of contraction and downgrading. The building was reduced in width, the timber walls encased in brick and finally it was abandoned altogether as a dwelling.

When the derelict building was discovered, various conservation plans were mooted, including removing it to St Fagans museum, but in the end the decision was made to restore Ty Mawr on its original site as a historic monument and a living house. Following lengthy restoration work the hall has been returned to its seventeenth-century appearance, while making allowances for modern requirements such as underfloor heating, discreet lighting and glass in the wooden window frames. In a further recognition of the outstanding importance of Ty Mawr, the house was awarded the accolade of Building of the Year 2000, ahead of such prestigious rivals as the Sydney Olympic Stadium and the Royal Opera House.

Access: Ty Mawr is owned by the Powis Castle Estate, and is open 10-12, 2-5, Fridays and Saturdays, June to September. It lies west of Welshpool. If approaching from the main Newtown road (A483) turn off to Berriew, pass through the village and take the B4385 turning to Castle Caereinion. After 5km you will see a large house on the right beside the entrance to a dead-end road. Take this turning and Ty Mawr will be reached after 1km (OS map ref: SJ 173 044).

Colwyn Bay *Llys Euryn*

Llys Euryn

Although only shattered stonework remains of Llys Euryn, our understanding of the site has been greatly enhanced by recent excavations and award-winning conservation work. The outer walls are largely intact and stand to full height in places, while the buried foundations of the vanished internal buildings have been exposed to view. This large house was built around the middle of the fifteenth century by Robin ap Gruffudd Goch, on the site of a manor once owned by Ednyfed Fychan, chief steward to Llywelyn, Prince of Wales.

Defensive considerations may have dictated the rather inward-looking design of the house, which consisted of mostly two-storeyed buildings ranged around three sides of an enclosed courtyard. All the internal walls were timber-framed and probably had large windows facing the courtyard, for elsewhere tiny loopholes seem to have been the norm, even on the upper floors. The great hall stood at the front and its cross-passage doubled as an access corridor to the courtyard and other buildings. By looking at the ruined walls it is still possible to make out the position of the windows, floor beams and upper chambers. Each side of the square building had lateral fireplaces and privy turrets, while the towering chimney on the far side belonged to a second hall added towards the end of the sixteenth century. Shortly thereafter the family fortunes took a downturn and the house gradually declined in importance, before being finally abandoned in the nineteenth century.

Access: The remains are freely accessible and form part of the Bryn Euryn nature reserve, just west of Rhos-on-sea. From the A55 at Colwyn Bay take the B5115 towards Penrhyn Bay and Llandudno. After 1.5km turn left at the traffic lights along Rhos road, and you will find the entrance to the nature reserve on the right. Park here, then walk back along the lane a short distance to where some steps lead up to the house (OS map ref:SH 833 801).

Conwy *Aberconwy House*

For years this was claimed to be the oldest house in Wales, reputedly built after Edward I established the castle and borough of Conwy in 1283 to crush the power of the Welsh princes. However, recent analysis of the main timbers produced a date ranging between 1417 and 1420, proving that Aberconwy House was built a few years after the troops of Owain Glyndŵr had swept through the walled town on their way to capture the castle.

Though not as old as previously thought, this is still a very respectable age and the house is fortunate to have survived at all when so many other historic buildings in Wales have gone for good. It is a rectangular three-storey block with rough masonry walls crowned by a timber-framed attic jutting out over the street on massive carved brackets. The original ground-floor shop is now a semi-basement, for the street level has risen by several feet over the years, giving the impression that the house has sunk into the ground through age and weight. On the first floor there is a kitchen and reception hall, while the top floor is divided into three rooms with attics above. In the medieval phase however, this was open to the roof. All the existing fireplaces are later modifications and it is unclear how the medieval house was warmed, but presumably there were hearths in the much altered rear wall.

Like any dwelling occupied continuously over a long period of time, Aberconwy House has undergone considerable changes as successive owners adapted the building to suit their tastes and requirements. In the eighteenth and early nineteenth centuries it was the residence of a merchant seaman, then in Victorian times the house was used as a temperance hotel. The National Trust has owned the property since 1934 and has carried out extensive renovation work, furnishing rooms to represent the various phases in its history. Most impressive of all is the open-roofed chamber on the topmost floor, which has been returned to its appearance as a wealthy merchant's home of the 1660s.

Aberconwy House

Cutaway reconstruction of Aberconwy House as it may have looked in the sixteenth century, before the attic was inserted into the upper chamber

Access: The house is open daily (except Tues) April-October 11-5. It stands on the corner of Castle Street within the historic walled town of Conwy, off the A55 between Bangor and Colwyn Bay (OS map ref: SH 781 776).

Crickhowell *Tretower Court*

The domestic architecture of six centuries is encapsulated at Tretower. An earth and timber castle was established around 1100, a stone keep built some 50 years later, and further masonry works added around 1250. As the age of the castle waned, an undefended manor house was built nearby and this was subsequently refurbished and extended into the eighteenth century.

Around 1450 Roger Vaughan, half-brother to the powerful William Herbert of Raglan Castle and an enthusiastic supporter of the Yorkist faction, acquired the Tretower estate. Both men were typical of the ruthless and self-seeking aristocracy that profited from the weakened government during the Wars of the Roses. Under the favour of the usurper Edward IV the two lords rose to prominence, William spending his wealth on rebuilding Raglan and Roger on Tretower. But the fluctuating fortunes of the Houses of York and Lancaster brought disasters as well as triumphs. William was executed by his opponents in 1469 and two years later Roger met the same fate. Tretower passed to his son Thomas, who embarked on a further scheme to give the house the appearance, if not the reality, of a fortified manor. The courtyard front was enclosed with a battlemented wall and a formidable-looking gatehouse – yet the back of the house was completely open to attack!

Tretower Court (see also photographs on pages 42 and 46)

Further work was carried out by Sheriff Charles Vaughan (d.1637) and his alterations can be detected in the liberal use of spacious glazed windows and the clusters of diagonal chimneys. The house remained with the Vaughan family until 1783 when it was sold off and relegated to the status of a farm. The decay was fortunately halted in the 1930s and the building has since been carefully restored.

Cutaway reconstruction of the great hall at Tretower, showing the impressive roof trusses and timber panelling. The courtyard was overlooked by a balcony extending across the front of the hall

From outside, Tretower Court appears virtually intact and still occupied, but inside all the rooms are empty and bare. Once through the gateway the visitor is confronted by the main front of the great hall. On the right-hand side there is a timber gallery at first-floor level, an unusual feature that formerly extended right around the courtyard, but was largely lost when Charles Vaughan gave the building a facelift in the seventeenth century. Within the hall many of the timber partitions that divided up the service end have gone, but the impressive full-height post-and-panel screen flanking the cross-passage is still here.

The long north wing is thought to be the earliest part of the house and contains basic storerooms on the ground floor, with guest accommodation above. Although the internal partitions have been taken down on this floor, slots and peg holes in the ornate roof trusses help to reconstruct the layout. There was a hall with three adjoining bedrooms, all provided with fireplaces and privies. Clearly the up-and-coming Vaughans expected to entertain the nobility at their home and the provision of comfortable, well-appointed chambers would have been taken for granted by status conscious guests. Some of the timbers have recently been tested to provide fairly accurate dates for the various parts of the Court. The hall trusses were shaped from trees cut down in 1447, the north wing was re-roofed around 1461 and the kitchen block in 1469. On this evidence work must have been in hand before Roger Vaughan acquired Tretower and he probably managed to see his grand home completed before his downfall.

Access: In the care of CADW and open to the public daily 10-4 between April and October. Tretower Court and castle lie 3 miles north-west of Crickhowell, just off the A40 Abergavenny to Brecon road (OS map ref: SO 186 212).

Llanberis *Cwm Brwynog hafotai*

In 1352 a survey was drawn up of the Welsh estates seized some years before by King Edward I, and among the sites included was a *hafod* settlement at 'Crombroinok'. This must surely be a reference to a group of long huts in Cwm Brwynog on the west flank of Eryri. A hafod was a temporary dwelling built by farmers and shepherds for use in the summer months, when cattle were taken for grazing in the uplands. Here in this cheerless rocky valley beneath the greatest mountain in Wales, can be found the remains of at least six rectangular stone buildings. They are all roughly the same size, measuring 3.2m by 7.8m internally, with tumbled drystone walls about 0.8m thick. One has the remains of a bench or sleeping platform across the upper end. The thatched roofs of the buildings have long since decayed away, leaving only their bare foundations like fossils in the landscape.

Access: Needless to say, you will need a lot of energy and enthusiasm to get to this site! The huts can be reached by following the well-marked footpath from Llanberis to the summit of Eryri. At Halfway Station veer down into the valley to your right and follow the fence line till it ends, where a stream crosses your way. The huts lie on a ridge beside this stream close to the valley bottom (SH 593 567).

Llansadwrn *Hafoty*

On an island particularly rich in ancient and historic monuments, the recently restored Hafoty must rank as one of the architectural glories of Anglesey. The gleaming white walls and tall chimneys stand proud on a rocky knoll beneath the shade of a monkey-puzzle tree. Although this was clearly a property of some status, very few records survive to illuminate its early history. In the fourteenth century it was known as *Bodiordderch* ('the dwelling of Iordderch') and it only gained its current name of *Hafoty* ('summer house') at the end of the seventeenth century. In the later medieval period the Norris family owned the estate and they were responsible for building the existing house.

From the outside Hafoty looks like a classic H-plan medieval house, with a central hall flanked by cross-wings at either end; but during recent conservation work experts realised that the building was far more complex than previously thought and only achieved its present form after many alterations. It seems likely that Hafoty began life as a box-framed hall, with a cross-wing at the upper end containing two ground-floor rooms and a large private chamber on the first floor. The walls were presumably built from clay, since no evidence for dismantled timber panels was noted in the surviving trusses. The date of the original house has not been established, but it could well have been built in the early fifteenth century. Some time elapsed before the owners decided to upgrade their home and replaced the clay walls with more durable masonry. The upper cross-wing was treated first, followed by the hall, and then another wing was added to the lower end of the hall, transforming a T-shaped layout into a H-plan. Both wings had the luxury of fireplaces and privy turrets.

Sometime in the sixteenth century the wealthy and influential Bulkeley family of Beaumaris acquired the property. This opportunity may have arisen due to the execution in 1536 of Henry Norris, who had been implicated in the downfall of Anne Boleyn. The Bulkeleys were here for a short time and the only mark of their tenure is the large fireplace in the hall, which replaced the open hearth and proudly bears their crest: *'If God be with us, who can be against us?'* In 1577 the first in a long succession of tenants moved in and only minor alterations occurred thereafter. When the last tenant moved out in the 1960s, the building became increasingly derelict and its future looked uncertain. However, CADW stepped in and carried out a lengthy process of excavation and renovation. The walls have been limewashed, the large Victorian windows replaced with traditional arched frames, decayed and missing timberwork renewed and finally, after years of conservation work, Hafoty has been restored to its sixteenth-century appearance.

Cutaway reconstruction of Hafoty, showing the hall and service rooms (left). Both cross-wings had privy turrets (which do not appear in the photograph opposite as they were later removed)

Access: Although the conservation of Hafoty has been completed, further work is needed before full public access can be allowed (contact CADW for further information). The house lies on farmland about 7km north of Menai Bridge, off the B5109 Beaumaris to Pentraeth road. If approaching from Beaumaris, pass Llansadwrn village and take the next right towards Llanddona. After 1km along this road, a lane on the left leads across the fields to the house (OS map ref: SH 563 783).

Machynlleth *'Owain Glyndŵr's Parliament House'*

What started in 1400 as a great patriotic rebellion and struggle for independence under an elected Welsh ruler ended with years of devastation and repression. The revolt of Owain Glyndŵr lasted a decade and left the English Crown reeling and the Welsh countryside ravaged and war-torn. At the height of his power Owain controlled much of the country and held native parliaments at Machynlleth and Harlech Castle. The ruins of the latter still dominate the countryside, but what do we have at Machynlleth? Is the plain stone hall in the centre of town the very building that once echoed to Owain's rallying cry?

Unfortunately not. Some vestiges may endure in the thick slate walls, but what remains today is essentially a large hall-house dating from the late fifteenth century (the main roof trusses have recently been dated to 1470). According to a brief description published in *Archaeologia Cambrensis* (1851) the old Parliament House had been 'taken down' some years before. By the beginning of the twentieth century whatever remained had been split up into two cottages, and in 1912 it was gutted and restored in an exuberant gothic style. From the few original features remaining inside, it is possible to conjecture that this building was a very long hall, with storeyed rooms at either end warmed by fireplaces in the end gables. There are vestiges of a cross-passage and some timber-framed partitions, but unfortunately the house has suffered so many alterations that the original layout is far from clear. Further restoration work was carried out in 1982 and the house now contains an exhibition on Owain and the native princes of Wales.

Access: The Parliament House is open daily between Easter and September and stands in Maengwyn Street, Machynlleth town centre (OS map ref: SH 747 009).

Magor *The Procurator's House*

A Procurator had the task of collecting rents and taxes from church-owned properties. The on-site information plaque at this ruined house claims a fourteenth-century date, but in fact the surviving architectural details are much later, probably *c.*1500. Most of the building has long gone (outlines of the foundations are marked on the grass), but the remaining fragments point to a lavish and well-appointed dwelling. It was referred to as a 'mansion house belonging to the vicarage' in 1585. Unlike many of the sites included in this section, The Procurator's House was not an open hall but an early example of the storeyed houses that were built in increasing numbers during the Tudor period. The plan consists of a rectangular block with a rear privy turret, and a large porch facing the parish church. Inside there was a dimly-lit basement and two residential upper floors replete

The Procurator's House, Magor

with spacious windows and lateral fireplaces. The porch has virtually disappeared, but it must have looked very much like the ornate one gracing the church a few feet away. Beside the car park in the village can be seen a fragment of another early house.

Access: The ruins are freely accessible and lie next to a public car park beside the church in Magor village, M4 junction 23a (OS map ref: ST 424 870).

Newborough *Llys Rhosyr*

Tradition had long identified this site as one of a number of Welsh medieval manors on Anglesey, but the actual remains were only discovered in 1992. A team from the Gwynedd Archaeological Trust began digging in a field beside Newborough church and uncovered the most complete *llys* yet recorded in Wales. During the Middle Ages the countryside was divided up into small territories controlled from a central *llys,* or royal court. Here at Rhosyr the foundations of four buildings have been exposed, dating from the reign of Prince Llywelyn in the thirteenth century. The main building was a rather modest hall with timber-framed walls on stone foundations and a thatched roof probably supported by crucks. Three smaller stone buildings stood close by, and one of them (perhaps a private chamber or parlour) was reached from the hall along a covered passageway. Surrounding everything was a well-built stone wall and a gate – not strong enough to keep an army out, but certainly sufficient to deter thieves and create an impressive feature. Had King Edward I left the Welsh alone, Llys Rhosyr might have grown and developed into a far grander medieval complex, but with the defeat of the native princes, the victorious English had no need of modest Welsh halls, and the site was neglected. It was only due to sandstorms in the 1330s that the slight remains were preserved underground for archaeologists to find more than six hundred years later.

Access: Llys Rhosyr is freely accessible and lies close to Newborough church, Anglesey. From the A5 follow signs to Newborough village then take the signposted road towards Llanddwyn. The preserved foundations lie in a field on the right, just where the road makes a sharp bend (OS map ref: SH 419 654).

Penarth *Cosmeston Medieval Village*

Like the Iron Age round houses at St Fagans and Castell Henllys, this is a group of buildings reconstructed from the ground up, using traditional methods and materials to recreate the probable appearance of a lost fourteenth-century village. The largest building formed a size-able farmstead with an adjoining barn and cowshed arranged around an open courtyard. Each house is basically a single rectangular room with an open hearth at one end, around which

Cosmeston village

the family sat, cooked and ate. Some of the rooms have been divided up by thin timber partitions, and loft spaces for storage and extra sleeping space have been built into the rafters. Furniture was sparse and very basic, just a few wooden benches and stools, and manger-like beds against the side walls. As such, they closely resemble cottages and peasant houses that were still being built in Wales five hundred years later. Apart from the domestic buildings the village has a number of restored agricultural buildings, including a barn, a dovecote, and a beehive-shaped pigsty, along with a thriving (and vociferous) community of farm animals.

Access: Cosmeston Country Park lies about 6km south-west of Cardiff and can be reached from the city by following the signs to Penarth, then taking the B4267 towards Sully. There are guided tours of the village daily 11-4 between March and November and special events are held during the summer months (OS map ref: ST 178 690).

Pwllheli *Penarth Fawr*

The rugged unprepossessing stone exterior of Penarth Fawr hides a 500-year-old secret; cross the immaculately kept garden, push open the heavy wooden door and you enter a latticework of dark timbers framing the empty, echoing grandeur of a medieval hall. Analysis of the woodwork has indicated that the house was built shortly after 1476, probably by a wealthy local landowner named Howel ap Madog, who combined local materials with architectural styles more commonly found further to the east.

The internal layout, however, is almost universal, with service rooms on two floors, a cross-passage, a central hall open to the roof and a further set of private rooms beyond the dais partition. These inner rooms were removed in the nineteenth century, making the house shorter than it should be. The approach to the hall is framed by a splendid carved spere-

The hall at Penarth Fawr

truss, which emphasised the wealth and status of the owner. The rest of the roof is no less impressive, with ornamental cusping and windbraces and a miniature truss designed to support the smoke vent above the central hearth. A timber canopy probably extended over the high table to stop ash and soot falling on the seated guests. This problem was solved completely in 1615, when Howel's descendant, Hugh Gwyn, replaced the archaic open hearth with a fine stone fireplace. His grandson John further altered the hall by inserting an upper floor into the roof space and greatly extending the house at the rear.

Thanks to restoration work in 1937, Penarth Fawr gives a good impression of the grandeur and spaciousness of a medieval hall, but little else – the flagstone floor and large glazed windows are wholly modern. In the fifteenth century Penarth would have been a gloomy, draughty, smoke-filled building with a rush-strewn earth floor and unglazed windows, lacking in hygiene, privacy and other amenities we now take for granted. But by medieval standards this was the sumptuous dwelling of a proud householder, and no doubt an object of envy to his less well-off neighbours.

Access: In the care of CADW and freely accessible. Penarth Fawr lies about 3 miles north-east of Pwllheli on the Lleyn Peninsula, and the route is clearly signposted from the A497 to Criccieth (OS map ref: SH 419 377).

Runston Deserted Medieval Village

On a low hill overlooking the Severn Estuary the gaunt ruins of St Kenya's church stand sentinel over the remains of a lost settlement. This is one of the best preserved deserted village sites in Wales and the stony foundations of over twenty houses can be seen. Runston was in existence by the thirteenth century, but it never thrived, and an estate map of 1772 indicates only six houses standing at the time. All have now gone.

Access: In the care of CADW and freely accessible. Runston lies 4km east of Chepstow off the A48 to Newport (M48 junction 2). On entering the village of Crick take the right turn to Shirenewton and then the next right after 1.5km. There is limited parking beside the buildings on the right, from where a public footpath crosses the fields to the church (OS map ref: ST 495 916).

Nantclwyd House, Ruthin

64

Ruthin *Nantclwyd House*

Opened to the public in 2007 after years of restoration work, this impressive timber-framed building is one of the oldest surviving houses in Wales. It has been added to, extended and altered, from the fifteenth to the twentieth century, and to celebrate changing domestic tastes over the years the interior rooms have been restored and furnished in a historic style that reflect the 'Seven Ages of Nantclwyd', from a medieval bedroom to a 1940s living room.

The house occupies a prime place between the market square and the gates of the thirteenth-century castle, and was doubtless built on the site of an older dwelling razed during the rebellion of Owain Glyndŵr (Ruthin was Owain's first target in the uprising). Timber analysis has pinpointed a construction date of 1435 or 1436 for the earliest phase of the surviving structure and (rare for a building of this status) there is even a contemporary record of the likely builder, a wealthy local weaver named Gronw ap Madog. Gronw and his English wife Suzanna owned two parcels of land in the town, which enabled their home to be constructed lengthwise to the main street, rather than the more usual end-on arrangement that narrow burgage plots allowed. Their fine new house was dominated by a central hall spanned by a single massive cruck-truss, not a typical continuous curving blade, but a much rarer jointed cruck made up of shorter lengths of timber spliced and pegged together. The spaciousness of the original hall can still be experienced today, despite the later fireplace and inserted gallery. There were probably storeyed rooms at either end of the hall, but only one of these suites survives and the upper floor has been recreated as a typical medieval bedchamber with a rather startling red and ochre colour scheme.

Another document refers to a later owner, John Holland, receiving permission in 1471 to cut down fourteen trees to build a cross-wing at one end of the house. This was swept away in the 1620s when the then occupier, Simon Parry, began the modernisation of the old hall-house. Parry was responsible for adding the north-west wing, which has an attractive open roofed chamber on the upper floor fitted out as a Jacobean merchant's room. The present day appearance of Nantclwyd is largely due to further extensive works carried out at the end of the seventeenth century by Eubule Thelwall, who notably added the attractive pillared entrance porch. The rear elevations are a mixture of stone and exposed timberwork representing yet again the many years of alterations carried out here. Behind the house the grounds extend to a large walled enclosure (formerly the kitchen garden of Ruthin Castle), overlooked by a restored eighteenth-century summer house.

Access: Nantclwyd is in the care of Denbighshire County Council and is open 10-5 Friday to Sunday, from April to the end of September. It lies in Castle Street, just off the main square in Ruthin town centre (OS map ref: SJ 124 582).

St Davids & Lamphey *The Bishop's Palaces*

During the Middle Ages the Bishops of St Davids Cathedral wielded power and spiritual authority over a vast swathe of land. Within the diocese there were many estates containing residences for the peripatetic prelate and his retinue, but the grandest of all was the *palacium*

The Bishop's Palace, St Davids, showing Bishop Gower's hall, the largest first-floor hall in Wales

at the cathedral city itself. That such a huge structure as this – stunning even in its ruin – was built at all says much about the wealth and prestige of the medieval church in Wales.

There must have been some sort of dwelling here from the early days of the cathedral and some parts of the existing ruin date back to *c.*1200, but it was during the rule of Thomas Bek (1280-93) and David Martyn (1293-1328) that the palace took on its present form. A long hall block was constructed facing the cathedral and, like most early stone buildings in west Wales, the principal rooms were on the first floor over dark, vaulted storerooms.

This building proved wholly inadequate for Martyn's successor, Bishop Henry de Gower (1328-47), who added an enormous second hall, measuring over 36m long. This huge building was probably used more for formal occasions and state functions than day-to-day living. In the gable end facing the cathedral is a fine rose window, devoid now of the stained glass that once flooded the interior with multi-coloured light. There was no fireplace, so the Great Hall must have been warmed by at least one open hearth, the smoke escaping through a vent in the high-pitched roof. Henry unified his new work with the old by remodelling the roofline and adding an elaborate parapet supported on a row of arches. An extra touch of refinement was provided by a chequered pattern of inlaid coloured stones.

Henry de Gower was an enthusiastic builder and his characteristic parapets also appear at **Lamphey** near Pembroke, a place where the bishop could relax and indulge in the lifestyle of a rich country gentleman. Here there were gardens, orchards, fishponds, barns, dovecotes and an extensive deer park. The buildings were arranged in a line to overlook the placid waters of the ponds and eventually included three first-floor halls, a large chapel and various ancillary buildings. The first hall was probably constructed around 1200 and then the larger Western Hall was built during the time of Bishop Carew (1256-80). Finally De Gower's eastern hall with its arcaded parapet was added around 1350. Some of the plaster clinging to the bare walls shows traces of painted decorations in the form of imitation stonework (a popular design in the fourteenth century).

At the Reformation Lamphey was sold off to the Devereux family and the young Robert (the future Earl of Essex and Queen Elizabeth's favourite) spent some of his teenage years here. By the late seventeenth century the lavish buildings had degenerated into a tenanted farm, and the site was in ruins by the following century. The palace at St Davids suffered the same fate. Bishop Barlow (1536-48) stripped the lead from the roof of the Great Hall and the remaining buildings lingered in use until terminal decay set in.

Access: Both sites are in the care of CADW and open standard hours. Lamphey lies 3km east of Pembroke off the A4139 to Tenby (OS map ref: SN 018 008). The palace at St Davids lies next to the cathedral at the westernmost tip of Wales, reached via the A487 from Haverfordwest (OS map ref: SM 750 253).

St Florence *Carswell House*

In total contrast to the palatial dwellings of the church hierarchy at St Davids and Lamphey, this tiny house was the home of a minor landowner – yet it too is a first-floor hall with a vaulted undercroft. No details survive at this roofless ruin to pinpoint a date, but it may have been built around 1500. The ground-floor room was the kitchen and has a huge fireplace in the end wall served by a typically massive Pembrokeshire square chimney. Access to the first-floor residential chamber was by an external wooden stair, which could have been withdrawn inside to increase security. The room itself is barely 5m square and has a fireplace and tiny unglazed windows. There is another minuscule defensible house at West Tarr a short distance away towards St Florence, although this is not yet open to the public. Elsewhere in Pembrokeshire other first-floor halls can be seen from the roadside at Penally, Lydstep and Flimston.

The Tudor Merchant's House, Tenby

Access: In the care of CADW and freely accessible. Carswell farm lies 4km west of Tenby. From the town follow the A4139 to Penally and take a right turn along a minor road to Trefloyne and St Florence. After about 3km the road bends sharply and there is a right-hand turning which leads down a narrow lane to the farm. Park outside the farm and cross the yard to the ruined house (OS map ref: SN 098 010).

Tenby *The Tudor Merchant's House*

Within the historic walled town of Tenby there are many old houses signalling their antiquity to the passer-by with archaic features that have just managed to avoid modernisation. Here and there are arched doorways, tall stone chimneys, and upper floors supported on jutting stone brackets. The Tudor Merchant's House was built around 1500 in one of the narrow lanes winding down from the church to the quay. We do not know who owned the house, but it was probably the residence of a wealthy merchant and his family as the traditional name suggests.

The plan is typical of town houses: a long narrow building running back from the street, with a small shop or workroom at the front and a side passage connecting with the rear rooms. All over the walls there are traces of faded paintings of seventeenth- or eighteenth-century date. The back room is a kitchen with a cavernous fireplace, served by an equally monumental chimney. A modern stair now climbs to the principal residential chamber on

A cutaway reconstruction of The Tudor Merchant's House, Tenby

the first floor, but it is clear that this fine room was originally entered by a separate stair and doorway in the side wall (as shown in the reconstruction drawing). A second wooden stair provides access to the bedrooms nestling under an upper-cruck roof.

In most domestic buildings prior to the nineteenth century sanitary arrangements were almost non-existent, but here the builder opted for an in-house privy turret similar to those found at castles and large mansions. Perhaps the neighbours viewed this convenient convenience with a certain amount of envy as they trudged to the cesspit with their chamber pots, but in truth, the privy was very unhygienic and lay right next to the kitchen. During restoration work in 1984 the Dyfed Archaeological Trust excavated the interior of the privy and found a wide range of evidence of the economy and eating habits of the owners: the seeds of strawberries, plums, apples and figs, and the bones of partridges, rabbits, sheep and fish (as might be expected given the town's maritime history). But despite the varied cuisine there was the unpleasant reality of daily life in the Middle Ages; the pit would have buzzed with flies, wool or hay would have served as toilet paper, the occupants suffered from intestinal worms, and rats scurried about the dark corners of the house.

Access: The house is owned by the National Trust and is open daily (except Wednesday) April-October. It is located in a narrow lane off Tudor Square, in the centre of Tenby town, Pembrokeshire (OS map ref: SN 135 004).

Wrexham *Plas Cadwgan*
Don't go looking for this house in Wrexham, for it is no longer there. Plas Cadwgan was an enormous building of medieval origin that grew and expanded over the centuries, but was shamefully demolished in 1967. Fortunately a few of the main timbers were salvaged and taken over the border into England, where they were re-erected at the Avoncroft Museum of Buildings. Here, beneath the shelter of a modern canopy, stands one of the most impressive cruck trusses ever recorded in Wales. The arching timbers rise more than 9m high and span a width of just over 6m. At the entry end of the hall stood a spere-truss with a balcony over the cross-passage. Only these few fragments were saved, but preserved in their sterile new setting they look more like dinosaur bones than the remains of a house.

Access: Avoncroft Museum lies just outside Bromsgrove in Worcestershire and is signposted off the A38 (M5 junction 5). This is the English equivalent of St Fagans and there are many more re-erected buildings here worth seeing.

Long huts and house platforms in upland Wales
Several thousand long huts and house platform sites can be found throughout the country, mainly in upland areas where they have suffered less damage from ploughing and stone-robbing. The following are just a handful of the more impressive and reasonably accessible sites; reference to the RCAHMW Inventories of Caernarfonshire, Anglesey and Glamorgan will reveal many more for the enthusiast to track down.

The prehistoric relics above **Rowen** (near Conwy) have already been mentioned on pages 27-28. Directly uphill of the Maen-y-bardd burial chamber are two long huts with associated enclosure walls and cultivation plots *(SH 741 721)*. A short distance further uphill beside a solitary thorn bush is another pair of huts. The largest measures 8.4m by 2.6m, and lies within a well-marked oval enclosure bounded by stone slabs. A few kilometres south beside **Pen-y-gaer** hillfort, an extensive settlement site can be traced alongside a footpath off the Llanbedr road *(SH 753 689)*. The remains of old boundary walls, animal enclosures, two ruined cottages and at least a dozen long huts can be found here. The site probably represents a settlement mentioned in fifteenth-century documents.

Archaeologists have recovered finds dating to the fifteenth and sixteenth centuries at a group of long huts in the **Brenig Valley**, near Denbigh *(SH 985 575)*. These were believed to be seasonal *hafotai* and the foundations can be seen from the heritage trail that skirts the edge of the Brenig reservoir (and which also passes close to some impressive Bronze Age monuments).

Travelling down south to **Cefn Drum** at Pontardulais *(centred at SN 61 04)*, some twenty platforms and long huts are scattered over the open hillside close to well-worn footpaths, although the summer undergrowth can hide much. The excavation of two platforms in 1996-8 revealed low walls of stones set in clay and central post-holes for supporting the roof. Subsequent exploration of a pair of long huts revealed that one was a dwelling, while the other was a sheepfold. Unfortunately no dating evidence was recovered. In contrast, the platforms on **Gelligaer Common** (near Merthyr) produced finds of late thirteenth- to early fourteenth-century date. Excavations here in the 1930s revealed the outlines of turf and rubble walls, with a central line of post holes for the roof supports. Over twenty platforms are scattered along the flanks of a broad ridge between the Bargoed and Rhymney valleys and the most accessible group lies about 600m east of the mountain road to Fochriw *(SO 115 027)*.

One more group in south Wales deserves to be highlighted here. In recent years archaeological surveys have been carried out on the Black Mountain and Forest Fawr stretching from Ammanford in the west to Merthyr Tydfil in the east. Numerous long huts have been found in the small stream valleys that drain the mountain flanks, though whether these were permanently occupied dwellings or seasonal *hafotai* is unclear. The stony foundations of huts with associated field walls can be found on the ridge above Dan-yr-Ogof *(SN 846 174)* and Nant Pennig beside the Beacons Reservoir *(SN 982 189)* (see photograph on p.32). The energetic rambler can discover many more in the upper reaches of the Twrch, Aman and Tawe valleys. A particularly good site can be seen conveniently from the A4069 Brynaman to Llangadog road *(SN 726 158)*, where the road bends sharply next to a lay-by. Look over the embankment down into the Garw valley and you will see a well-marked hut in a crook of the stream. A short distance upriver at **Tro'r Derlwyn** is a more prominent hut with two adjoining drystone pens. Excavations here indicated that the site was occupied as late as the eighteenth century.

PART THREE

1550 - 1800

The Reformation and beyond

King Henry VIII's break with the Church of Rome in the 1530s signalled more than the destruction of the monasteries of England and Wales. A whole mode of life was swept away. No longer could churchmen depend on the wealth brought in by pilgrims to shrines and holy sites. Confiscated property was sold off to the aristocracy to feed the king's insatiable appetite for money. For some this transition may not have seemed so great at first, since many monasteries had already leased out their vast tracts of land to tenant farmers. But the various changes wrought by the Reformation, along with the firm, stable government of the Tudor dynasty, had a major effect on the evolution of rural housing.

The spark that flamed this architectural revolution was an economic curse we are all too familiar with today – inflation. During the course of the sixteenth century inflation increased dramatically, bringing misery and suffering to some, but lucrative gains to others. Many landowners were living on long-term or fixed leases, so they were able to benefit from the increasing price of their produce without having to pay higher rents. More land was developed to achieve bigger surpluses to satisfy the needs of a rapidly growing population. The money gained was invested in 'bricks and mortar' and Britain became, quite literally, a building society. However, in such a competitive market, only those of a higher standing with the necessary cash and initiative benefited.

The social and economic conditions prevalent in Tudor times allowed for the widespread replacement of impermanent dwellings with more permanent ones. Historians have called this event the 'Great Rebuilding'. The movement reached a peak between the Act of Union (1536), when Wales was formally united with England, and the Civil War (1642). By studying the distribution pattern of early houses, experts have shown that it spread across the country from east to west, 'like ripples in a pond, the centre of which was metropolitan England', as Peter Smith put it.

In reality, the Great Rebuilding was not quite the clear-cut event it was thought to be when the concept was first proposed in the 1950s. Rebuilding took place in different areas of the country at different times; in the shires of Carmarthen and Cardigan for instance, the evidence points to a rebuilding phase well into the eighteenth century, while it could be argued that Wales had already witnessed a Great Rebuilding in the aftermath of the Glyndŵr rebellion. Even within the regions that retain a large number of early houses, there may be local differences between the building periods. A recent survey of Glamorganshire by the RCAHMW revealed a marked discrepancy between the houses of the agriculturally rich Vale (where the rebuilding started early in the sixteenth century) and the bleaker uplands (where the buildings are predominately of seventeenth-century date). Despite these regional variations, there is no doubt that the century between 1550 and 1650 witnessed a huge surge of house building across much of Britain.

From hearth to fireplace

The most significant change to affect house design in the course of the sixteenth century was the replacement of an open hearth with a fireplace and chimney. It could be said that when

Elizabeth I came to the throne in 1558 most people were living in a hall-house warmed by a hearth; but by her death in 1603 the majority of houses had at least one fireplace. An Essex rector of the 1570s commented how the old folk of his village marvelled at 'the multitude of chimneys lately erected, whereas in their young days there were not above two or three, if so many … but each made his fire against a reredos [stone screen] in the hall, where he dined and dressed his meat'. We have already seen how fireplaces were common in upper-class stone buildings such as castles, first-floor halls and town houses (where fire hazards necessitated such features from an early period). Even some hall-houses dating from the end of the Middle Ages had stone fireplaces. But it became increasingly commonplace for a house to be provided with at least one fireplace and this in turn meant that the lofty space of the hall (so necessary to allow smoke from a hearth to rise) was no longer needed.

At first, old buildings were adapted to new layouts. A stone or brick fireplace could be built within the framework of a timber hall with a minimum of fuss and then hefty beams thrown across the roof space to create an upper floor. A great many halls which were adapted in this hybrid fashion survive today, and it is only by stripping away the accumulated layers of modifications and adaptations, that historians can unravel the architectural history of a building. Incredible as it may seem, some people actually grumbled about the domestic improvements taking place. The mathematician Edward Howes wrote in 1632: 'I like well the old English [way of] building where the room is large and the chimney or hearth in the middle. Certainly thereby ill vapour and gnats are kept out, less fuel will serve the turn, and men had more lusty and able bodies than they have now'!

As the fireplace supplanted the hearth, so its location within the house led to the adoption of new layout plans and interior designs. The old arrangement of outer room / hall / inner room was still very popular, but now that a chimney superseded the central hearth, the problem facing the builders was where to put it. The earliest attempts opted to set the fireplace in one of the side walls, creating what is termed a *lateral chimney* house (*Figure A*). This arrangement caused the least disruption to the traditional internal layout and found particular favour with the upper classes

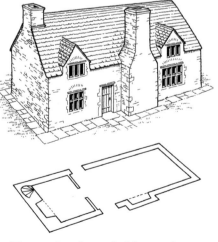

Figure A: a lateral chimney house

Aberbran-fawr (Brecon), a sixteenth-century lateral chimney house extended in 1746

(perhaps because the massive chimney was viewed as something of a status symbol). **Hafoty** and **Penarth Fawr** are medieval halls with added lateral chimneys, while at **Tretower** and Cochwillan they are original. Houses with lateral chimneys are found in great numbers in the old shires of Flint and Denbigh, with smaller concentrations in Glamorgan and Pembrokeshire.

Hearth-passage houses

A more popular place to put the chimney was backing against the cross-passage, so that the fireplace lay at the lower end of the hall warming the occupants seated at the upper (dais) end. This is known as a 'chimney backing on the entry' plan, but a less cumbersome term is a *hearth-passage* house (*Figure B*). This plan can be found all over Wales except in the extreme west and north, but the heaviest concentration is in the south-eastern shires from Monmouth to Carmarthen. Generally the internal layout remained the same, with the outer rooms occupying the space behind the new fireplace. Quite often there was an additional chimney in the gable wall warming the outer room. In its largest form a hearth-passage house might consists of three heated parts – a kitchen (the former outer room), a central hall, and a parlour (the old inner room). Those without the necessary cash opted for much smaller dwellings lacking an outer room, so that the fireside doorway is in an external gable wall. These are classed as *end-entry* houses and, although limited in size, they must have been deemed sufficient for the needs of the less affluent members of the farming community. **Kennixton** (now at St Fagans) was one of the smallest, one room up, one room down; but like many such houses it was enlarged at a later date. Most end-entry houses have two rooms on the ground floor, the main hall, and a smaller inner room which may or may not have been provided with a fireplace as well (*Figure C*).

The most famous member of the hearth-passage group is the long-house, an ancient form of dwelling where farmers and their animals lived under the same roof. Many of the long huts mentioned in the previous

Figure B: a hearth-passage house

Figure C: an end-entry house

Figure D: long-house with central chimney

section were probably dual-purpose dwellings and even some high-status halls like Middle Maestorglwydd and **Ty Mawr** had provision for cattle within the building. As the name suggests, a long-house is an elongated building divided into a dwelling part and a cattle shed. In the medieval period the cross-passage served as a communal entrance passage separating the two halves, although by the sixteenth century the introduction of a central chimneystack created a more substantial partition (*Figure D*). Llanerch-y-cawr near Rhayader is a good example of an upland long-house and one that has recently been restored from a derelict state. The whitewashed stone walls enclose an early sixteenth-century cruck hall modified in 1589 by the addition of a fireplace and upper floor. Another hall-house conversion is **Cilewent** (now at St Fagans), although here the fireplace is unusually positioned in the end gable wall and the cowshed is separated by a light timber partition (as indeed, it must have been in the medieval phase).

The cowsheds are invariably situated at the lower, or downhill end of the building for obvious reasons, yet strangely a handful of long-houses in the Afan valley in West Glamorgan were built with the cowshed at the *upper* end. This must have caused some interesting drainage problems. It was said that the occupants only took their boots off when getting into bed!

Much ink has been spilt over the years concerning this class of building and its relationship to other house types. There is an enduring misconception that any dwelling with an attached byre is a long-house, but in fact for a building to belong to this category the

Llanerch-y-cawr near Rhayaer, Powys, a sixteenth-century upland long-house

dwelling end must have been entered originally from the cowshed. Furthermore, studies have shown that many were built in two phases (an end-entry house coming first, then the cowshed added later). Most of the Carmarthenshire long-houses described by Iorwerth Peate as archetypal examples were clearly two-phase buildings. A plausible explanation for this piecemeal development is that a farmer would construct the living quarters first and only when more money was available would the adjoining cowshed be rebuilt in more durable materials.

Few long-houses remain today in their original state. More convenient entrances were invariably constructed in later years to avoid the messy process of entering the house through the byre, and many cowsheds have been turned over to domestic use. It is a sad fact that the least altered buildings are those now abandoned or in ruins, no-one having salvaged them for occupation in this day and age.

Lobby-entry houses

The next plan to consider is the *lobby-entry*. Here the chimney is positioned right in the centre of the cross-passage instead of to the side (*Figure E*). Thus sited, it rendered the passageway obsolete, but created efficient circulation space between the hall and outer room. Anyone entering such a house would open the door and face a blank wall, which is why this plan is known in some parts of Britain as a 'baffle-entry'. The stronghold of the lobby-entry house is mid Wales and the borders, and here the massive central stack usually has back-to-back fireplaces warming the rooms on either side. In other parts of the country a variant form is encountered, where fireplaces in the gable walls serve the end rooms, instead of a central stack. And just like the hearth-passage plan, lobby-entry houses can also be found in the diminutive end-entry form.

Talgarth (Trefeglwys), an example of a lobby-entry house with central chimney stack

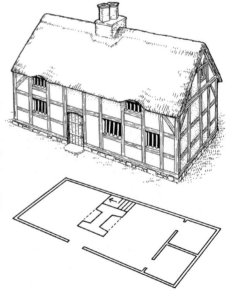

Figure E: a lobby-entry house

Direct-entry houses

The last house plan to examine is the *direct-entry*, so called because the front doorway leads straight into the hall (*Figure F*). There is usually an outer room behind a partition at the entry side, and a few houses even had an additional partition closing off the cross-passage from the hall, no doubt improving privacy and cutting down draughts. With this plan the main fireplace is positioned in the end gable *behind* the dais, a very awkward position in a traditional hall, since it would render the high table obsolete. The lateral-chimney houses mentioned above also belong to this group.

The direct-entry house is the most widespread and common of all plans, since it was used well into modern times. However, there are few examples built before 1700 and they are largely concentrated in the mountainous areas of the north-west (which is why they are sometimes termed 'Snowdonia houses'). **Garreg Fawr** from Waunfawr (now reconstructed at St Fagans)

Figure F: a direct-entry house

shows all the main features of this class, including the massive boulder walls, round-headed doors and fortress-like windows so typical of the region.

These then, are the main house plans that were in use between the sixteenth and eighteenth centuries – the direct-entry (both gable chimney and lateral chimney type), the hearth-passage, and the lobby-entry. (Research has brought to light two other distinct house types – 'gable-entry' and 'offset-entry' – but these are very few in number and mainly restricted to the south-east.) As we have seen there are regional preferences for each and a wide date range within which they were built. Their origins can be traced back

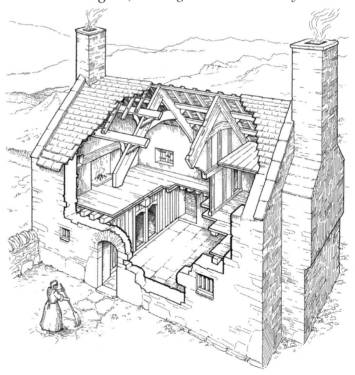

A cutaway reconstruction of Garreg Fawr, originally at Waunfawr, but now reconstructed at St Fagans

A cutaway reconstruction of Pen-y-ddol, Trefeglwys, a medieval cruck hall that had a chimneystack and upper floor inserted

to medieval halls converted into storeyed houses by adding upper floors and chimneys. But even as this conversion process was going on, many more houses were being built to entirely new plans, without ever having originated as an open hall. We can see this by looking at two examples: Pen-y-ddol and Middle Gaer. Pen-y-ddol (Trefeglwys) is a typical medieval cruck hall that was altered by having an upper chamber and chimneystack inserted. As with many such conversions it was none too successful, since the crucks severely limited the headroom on the new first floor. In contrast, Middle Gaer (Tretower) was built around the middle of the sixteenth century as a storeyed house from the start, with two full-height storeys and attics. It has a hearth-passage plan and still retains the traditional three-unit layout. Houses of this period are sometimes classed as *sub-medieval*, because they still share the basic layouts and details of their medieval predecessors.

As years went by and money became available, the growing household might wish to extend the family home. A few rooms would be added in a small extension, or even a completely new wing built. Some landowners went further, adding two, three, or even four self-contained houses in the same farmyard. This duplication of dwellings is known

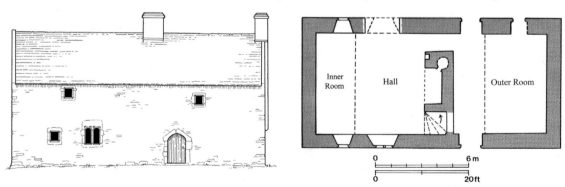

Middle Gaer, Tretower, built as a storeyed house on the hearth-passage plan in the middle of the sixteenth century

Berain, near Denbigh showing the addition of a new block on the left to the original hall house on the right

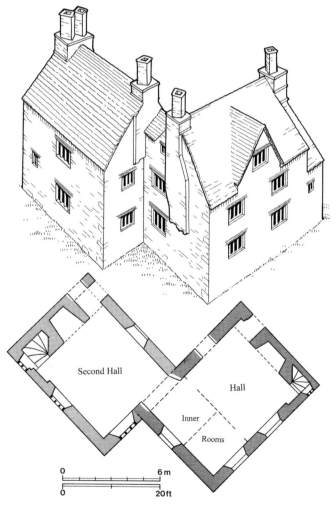

Second Hall

Hall

Inner

Rooms

0   6 m

0   20 ft

Plan and reconstruction of the White Hart, Llangibby

as the 'unit system', and it is an arrangement that can be found all over Britain. The unit system was first identified in the 1940s when survey work at Llanfrothen in north Wales revealed three houses linked together, with a fourth doubling as a stable and servant's quarters. The more usual arrangement is two houses side by side, or joined together, but self-contained, not merely extensions to an existing building. A good example is the White Hart at Llangibby near Usk. This roadside inn consists of two almost identical houses joined together at the corner. One house was built to a hearth-passage plan around 1600, while the second lobby-entry wing was added a few generations later. Berain (near Denbigh) is another example; here a detached tower-like block with accommodation on three floors supplemented the original hammer-beam hall-house. The style and quality of the second building suggests that it was built for the remarkable Catherine of Berain (*c*.1534-91), cousin to Queen Elizabeth I and the ancestress of several major Welsh families (she gained the sobriquet 'mam Gymru' through her four marriages and numerous offspring).

This duplication can also be seen on a much larger scale at the Bishop's Palaces at **Lamphey** and **St Davids**, and also at **Old Beaupre**. Experts think that the unit system arose where partible inheritance had split a family into two households. The farmstead would be run jointly by the heirs, but each family had their own house to live in. There is also evidence that some secondary dwellings were dower houses, where the widow of the landowner would live out her days while her offspring resided in the 'big' house.

Town houses

Generally speaking there was little architectural difference between a country house and a town house except for one inevitable factor – available space. Within the boundaries of an urban settlement or the claustrophobic confines of a walled town, there was less land available for expansive building, and most properties jostled for position along the main commercial streets. Since medieval times settlements had been planned with narrow burgage plots lining the streets. The house or shop stood at the front, with a long rear garden extending behind. Over the centuries these building plots became fossilised in the townscape, even though the houses themselves were subject to continual rebuilding and modernisation. Because of this repeated development town houses rarely survive unaltered compared to their rural counterparts, and some towns – in particular Cardiff, Swansea and Newport – have been so transformed that you could well think them wholly modern.

Within the space limits imposed by busy commercial centres, the builders still employed the traditional plans. A house would often be built end-on to the street, with a shop or workroom at the front, and an access corridor at the side (in place of the old cross-passage) leading to the hall or private chambers at the rear. This is the layout we see at the **Tudor Merchant's House** in Tenby. Where people couldn't build out, they built up; multi-storey buildings with two, three or even four upper floors became the norm in busy towns and cities, each level jutting out over the street on massive timber beams or brackets. **Aberconwy House** occupies a restricted corner plot within the defended town of Conwy, and therefore the only way to build the residential apartments was to stack them on top of the ground-floor shop.

The George and Dragon, Beaumaris

Nevertheless, the surviving evidence appears to suggest that most Welsh towns did not suffer from overcrowding and that there was sufficient space to allow for more expansive buildings. While many houses faced end-on to the street, others were built side-on, perhaps because the owner had acquired the adjoining burgage plot and merged the two properties into one. The George and Dragon (Beaumaris) is a typical example; now a public house, this was originally a substantial timber-framed building divided into several rooms or shops on the ground floor, with very fine residential apartments on the upper floor. In contrast, the charming little Tudor Rose, a short distance away in Castle Street, was originally an H-plan medieval hall built end-on to the road. All that now survives is the front cross-wing and some roof timbers of the hall.

The Tudor Rose, Beaumaris

Southern towns like Haverfordwest, Pembroke and Tenby were primarily built from stone and contained a large number of first-floor halls. Although the main accommodation has invariably been modernised, the solidly built vaulted undercrofts still survive in great numbers. In the north and west of the country the townscapes are predominately timber-framed. Places such as Newtown, Ruthin, Welshpool and Wrexham still retain half-timbered houses but, as noted earlier, extensive rebuilding in the nineteenth and twentieth centuries has considerably changed the appearance of these historic centres. Sometimes only travellers' accounts and early drawings reveal what has been lost.

Timber-framed hearth-passage house in Ruthin

81

A typical seventeenth-century house

Having discussed the plans of these 'new' storeyed houses, let us look inside a typical example to find out what home comforts meant for the seventeenth-century Welshman. My choice of a house to explore is Tynewydd, in my home town of the Rhondda. This relatively large house of hearth-passage plan is situated deep in the upland valleys of Glamorgan and must have been considered a palace by neighbouring standards when first built. On the prestigious entrance porch there is an inscribed stone bearing the incomplete date 16–2. Examination of the timber details suggests a mid seventeenth-century date, so the inscription should probably read 1652. Tynewydd means 'New House', and if the suggested date is correct, it was built in the aftermath of the Civil War and just three years after Charles I had lost his head. We know that the Edwards family owned the estate and the name of Morgan Edwards appears in the Hearth Tax survey of 1670; he may therefore have been responsible for building the existing house.

Once through the porch you enter the kitchen with its huge fireplace in the end wall containing two separate bake ovens (one is a portable clay oven made in Devon, which must have been brought here from one of the ports on the Glamorgan coast). This was the busiest room in the house, where the cook prepared food for the household: stew or thick pottage simmered in a cauldron over the fire, meat roasted on spits, hunks of bacon slowly cured in the smoky shaft of the chimney. Cheese and butter would be made and stored in the cool north-facing room at the back of the kitchen.

Seventeenth-century life in Tynewydd, the Rhondda. This shows the hall

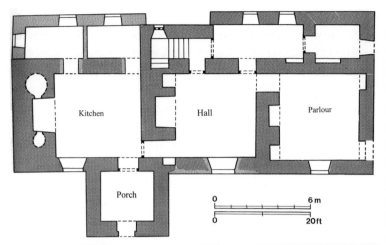

Down a short passageway alongside the central fireplace, you enter the hall. The oak ceiling here is more elaborate than in the kitchen, with carved principal beams and smaller joists set at right angles. Furniture was still sparse in this period. Apart from a heavy trestle table set at the head of the room there might have been a large chair reserved for the head of the household, a few stools or moveable benches, perhaps a wooden chest for storage, and a cupboard for displaying prized pewterware. Food was usually eaten off wooden or earthenware plates. Candles and rush lamps provided feeble illumination, but the plain limewashed walls served to brighten up the interior (in some houses even the ceiling beams were whitened). Beyond the high table a door led into a

A plan and photograph of Tynewydd

parlour with its own fireplace and the added refinement of a plaster ceiling.

In one corner of the hall, a door opens onto a dogleg stairway rising to the bedchambers on the upper floor. Half way up on the landing is the only original window now surviving in the house, and from the style of the wooden frame it seems that the owners were wealthy enough to afford glass. The main windows would have been filled with oblong panels of glass pieces set in lead strips, fixed by wires to the central metal bars of the frame, so that the panels could be removed if the family moved on – such was the value of glass in the seventeenth century! The first floor was divided up into three chambers plus a cosy little bedroom above the porch with its own fireplace. In earlier times sleeping arrangements were very primitive, consisting mainly of wooden platforms covered with straw mattresses, set as close to the fireplace as possible; but when Tynewydd was built it was quite common to have designated sleeping chambers, with elaborate wooden bed-frames and comfortable feather mattresses. The stair rose to the attic where there were three more rooms – unheated, dark and with limited headroom under the great oak trusses – but even these would have been used for storage and servants' accommodation.

Stone winding stairs beside the fireplace at Ffynnon Dwym (Rhondda)

Tynewydd is a fairly commodious house built by someone who chose to express his standing in stones and mortar, but many hill farms in the uplands of Wales were very much smaller. Some distance further east, near Pontypool in the neighbouring county of Monmouthshire, is Tal-ochor farm. This is typical of the many end-entry houses in this region and probably dates from around 1600. There is no grand porch as at Tynewydd, just a doorway in the gable wall leading straight into the hall; but the beamed ceiling is just as elaborate and an equally cavernous inglenook warms the room. Across the upper end of the hall there is an oak post-and-panel screen, with two doors at either end leading into a pair of inner rooms. One of the little rooms was a parlour, and the other (on the cooler north-facing side) a dairy.

Beside the fireplace a narrow stone stair rises in a half circle to the bedroom. Such winding stairs are almost universal in south-east Wales and remained a feature of domestic architecture into the early nineteenth century. Unlike the spacious bedrooms at Tynewydd, there is only a single chamber with limited headroom and two massive oak trusses holding up the stone-slated roof. Here the whole family slept; there was no privacy, no fireplace, and just one draughty unglazed window in the end wall. Nevertheless, this was not some squalid peasant dwelling. Tal-ochor was one of many substantial little houses built by the thriving farming communities in these remote valleys.

In the closing years of the eighteenth century, William Coxe (1747-1828) travelled through this part of Monmouthshire and left a rare description of the area before the Industrial Revolution had fully taken hold. His account of Ebbw Vale bears more resemblance to rural mid Wales than the overdeveloped landscape familiar to many people today. He saw 'numerous farm houses, with small inclosures of corn and pasture [occupying] the slopes ... the whitened walls and brown stone roofs of these detached dwellings, gave an air of neatness and gaiety to the surrounding landscape'. Further down the valley Coxe referred again to the striking appearance of the houses, whitewashed 'both within and without', and was equally impressed with the large quantities of bacon hanging from the kitchen ceilings. 'Bacon is almost the only meat served at the tables of the farmers, and with vegetables and the productions of the dairy, form their diet. Thin oat cakes are a common substitute for bread, and their repasts are enlivened with the cwrw'. Mutton, beef and pork would occasionally appear on the menu, along with cereals and dairy produce. Oatmeal pottage was a staple feature of the dinner table. This monotonous diet was the lot of most people because farms had to be self-sufficient and rely on what could be grown or produced locally. Only the wealthy could afford luxury foodstuffs and imported spices.

Coxe's description is something of a rarity, since few written accounts at this time mention traditional Welsh houses, but inventories, wills and parish registers provide a basic idea of the fixtures and furnishings present in the homes of this period. Beds, clothes and window glass seem to have been the most valued possessions

An unglazed timber window at Ty Hwnt y Bwlch (Cwmyoy)

handed down through the generations. When Blanche Powell of Monmouth compiled her will in 1582 she listed three feather beds, 'one in the parlour, one in the chamber over the parlour, the third in the kitchen'– clearly most rooms in her house would double for sleeping space. A specific reference to 'all the glass in the windows' is another reminder of the value of glazing at this time. And again, when William Jones of Usk made his will in 1591 he carefully stated that his wife was to receive the 'house where I now dwell, with all the wainscot and glass and the two beds and furniture in the great chamber and white chamber'. Further information about domestic standards is obliquely provided by the Hearth Tax returns of the 1660s (an inventive attempt by the government of the day to extract money from the people). The surveys reveal that the majority of houses in Wales only had one fireplace. If your home had three or more, you were well on your way up the social ladder, and could afford to keep the taxman happy. Today, to experience something of the quality of life in the seventeenth century, you could visit the period furnished houses at St Fagans Museum, Greenfield Valley Heritage Park or the more theatrical environs of **Llancaiach Fawr**.

The Renaissance and the great houses of Wales

Even as these new storeyed houses were spreading across the country, the first indications of a further change in architectural style began to appear. The Renaissance, which involved the rediscovery and application of the classical ideals of ancient Greece and Rome, first flourished in the artistic capitals of Europe, and in architectural terms led to a more formalised approach to buildings and an increase in external ornamentation. Proportion, balance and symmetry were the ideals sought after. Whereas all the houses previously described were built in the vernacular tradition (that is, by local craftsmen and apprentices relying on skills passed down through the generations), the hand of the professional architect is far more evident in Renaissance buildings. These changes were felt among the upper classes at first, particularly those who had court connections or had travelled abroad and witnessed the developments at first hand. It was to take some time for the ideas to filter down to the middle classes.

Most of the home-owning population of Wales was too poor and conservative to embrace these new concepts wholeheartedly, but while the traditional plans continued to be built, local craftsmen started to incorporate certain elements of the Renaissance style into their work. There was a greater emphasis on the façade; walls might be enriched with

Plasauduon, Carno, a Renaissance-style lobby-entry house with storeyed porch and rear service rooms

dressed stone pillars, classical mouldings and cornices; windows were arranged more symmetrically in the frontage; and rows of dormers illuminated attic rooms and created a more interesting roofline. As glass became cheaper and more widely available, the shape of windows changed from the low, wide medieval openings to tall frames with vertical and horizontal glazing bars. Heraldic plaques and date inscriptions became increasingly popular, and even chimneys might be clustered together or set diagonally (rather than squared to the gable) to provide a decorative flourish.

The most notable feature to appear in middle-class houses at this time was the storeyed porch. Originating in castle architecture, the grand porch appeared first in gentry houses and then rapidly spread through all the home-owning classes. Porches served to emphasise the main entrance and create a dramatic façade, as well as providing some extra accommodation in the chambers over the gate.

The above-mentioned Tynewydd displays some of these new features, as does **Plas Mawr** – arguably the finest early Renaissance house surviving in Wales. It was built in the period 1576-85 and some of its details were inspired by the work of Sir Richard Clough (*c.*1530-70), an

Plas Mawr

86

influential figure in the development of the Renaissance style in Wales. Clough was a local boy who made his fortune working in Antwerp. On his return to Wales and marriage to the wealthy heiress Catherine of Berain in 1567, Richard built two houses near Denbigh in the style and materials fashionable in the Low Countries. The first of these, Bachegraig, a bizarre cube-like building with a pyramidal roof crowned with a cupola, no longer survives, although it inspired a few similar oddities (such as Trimley Hall, Ffrith, built in 1653 on a hilltop near Leeswood and recently restored). Far more influential was Clough's choice of brick for the walls of Plas Clough, which reintroduced this material into Wales for the first time since the days of the Romans. Ironically the walls of Plas Clough are now rendered, but in any case, thanks to the ubiquitous modern use of brick, we are perhaps dulled to the striking impression this house must have made when completed over four centuries ago. Another imported feature of Plas Clough was the crow-stepped gable (a common sight in the Netherlands), which impressed Sir Richard's neighbours enough to set a vogue for the style across north Wales. Apart from these details the house is remarkably conventional, and has a central hall flanked by long wings extending to the rear, forming a U-shaped layout.

Crow-stepped gable at Plas Mawr (below), and as seen on a Dutch house (above)

The gentry of Elizabethan and Stuart Wales had plenty of money to spend on oversized houses that proclaimed to all and sundry just how wealthy and important they were. At first the houses were built to the traditional plans, but on a much larger scale and with sufficient rooms to accommodate the gentry in the manner to which they were accustomed. Thus **Llancaiach Fawr** is a typical lateral-chimney house, but with over a dozen rooms on three floors plus attics. Pencoed Castle (Llanmartin) shares the same basic plan but is much larger and has even more rooms for guests and retainers. Most amazing of all is **Oxwich Castle**, where just one tower-like wing contains six floors of bedrooms. For most the glory lasted only a short time, for when the owners sold up, moved on or died out, their successors rarely had the means to keep the buildings going. In Glamorgan alone there are over a dozen ruined great houses that failed to survive in more cash-conscious

Old Beaupre, Cowbridge

times. **Old Beaupre**, **Oxwich Castle, Neath Abbey** and Boverton Place (Llantwit Major) are still impressive even in their shattered state. Dilapidated Sker on the windswept coast near Porthcawl very nearly went the same way, but has recently undergone extensive restoration work. Onetime home of the Turberville family and incorporating the remains of a medieval monastic farm, Sker was built around 1580 and featured a grand first-floor hall with spacious windows and decorative plaster ceilings. An attempt was made to create a symmetrical

Sker House, near Porthcawl

Boverton Place, Llantwit Major

façade, but the rear elevation is a hodgepodge of wings, turrets and chimneys. Unfortunately, funds fell short of saving the ruined south wing so that the front now looks a little lopsided; nevertheless, this is a marvellous restoration and an encouragement for potential future projects. Many other historic buildings have not been so fortunate as Sker; Thomas Lloyd's *The Lost Houses of Wales* indicates the tragic scale of such losses.

If the gentry wanted to impress, they usually looked into their not-too-distant past and found something suitable in the age of the feudal strongholds. Courtyards were enclosed with battlemented walls, wings grew into tower-like structures and doorways were overburdened with fortified gatehouses. Such fancy dress costumes were applied to **Old Beaupre, Oxwich, Plas Mawr,** Pencoed Castle and Boverton Place, to name but a few. Allt-y-bella near Usk has recently been restored from a state of almost total collapse (it was even included as a casualty in Thomas Lloyd's book) and aptly demonstrates the Renaissance penchant for incongruous buildings. The main part of the house is a long low cruck-hall of modest proportions, but in 1599 Roger Williams added a tower-like residential block to one end. This tower contains three floors and an attic, all linked by a wooden spiral stair rising an extra storey. An attractive cluster of diagonal chimneys crowns the roof. This mock-medieval style reached its apogee in the hugely ambitious mansions of Rhiwperra (near Caerphilly) and Plas-teg (Hope). Both houses were built by court officials in the early seventeenth century and combined the towered façade of the old castles with all the comforts a Jacobean magnate would expect.

The extrovert changes to the outside of the building were mirrored by interior changes. There was a conscious desire for greater privacy and more efficient circulation between rooms. A typical example of this is highlighted by Dolbelydir

Rhiwperra near Caerphilly

(Trefnant), a late sixteenth-century house recently saved from dereliction by the Landmark Trust. Dolbelydir lies in the Vale of Clwyd and was the home of the scholar Henry Salesbury (c.1561-1605), author of the first Welsh grammar book. It was built around 1578 and shares many features with the traditional architecture of old Denbighshire – tall chimneys, off-centred windows, an imposing first-floor chamber with an arch-braced roof – but what is most notable about Dolbelydir is that the entrance does not open onto a cross-passage or lead directly into the hall, but instead gives access to a lobby and service room occupying the space between the hall and the kitchen. This early attempt at centralised circulation can also be found at **Ty Mawr** (Wybrnant) and the north wing of **Plas Mawr**.

Soon, however, this layout was vastly improved as builders dragged the stair out of the obscure corner it had hitherto occupied and gave it a major role to play. It could be said that as the fireplace revolutionised house plans in the sixteenth century, the stair did the same in the seventeenth. In Elizabethan mansions the stair was usually arranged in straight flights around a stone pillar or, if built entirely built from timber, rose up around a central void (the stairwell). This structure was generally housed in a turret projecting from the back of the building and could achieve quite massive proportions – at Gelli-dywyll (Blackwood) the stair wing is about as large as the house itself – which says more about the aspirations of the owner than the practical need to get upstairs! Before long the stair was relocated to a more convenient passageway within the building itself, thus creating the most important and far-reaching development of the Renaissance period, the *centrally-planned* house **(Figure G)**. Suites of rooms accessed from the central passage replaced the older arrangement of rooms in a line opening into each other.

The earliest example of this plan in Wales is believed to be Tyfaenor (Abbey Cwm-hir), which was built around 1656.

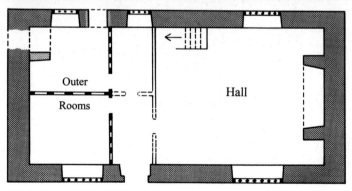

Plan and photograph of Dolbelydir, Trefnant, near Denbigh

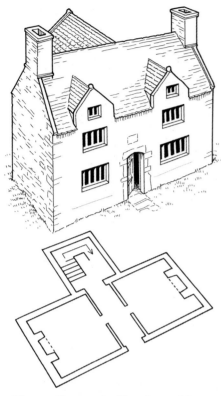

It is a rectangular stone block with gable fireplaces warming two rooms of equal size, separated by a central corridor containing the entrance lobby and stairwell. This layout was repeated on the upper floors and due to the sloping ground, there was a basement level with its own entrance allowing servants to move around the house without disturbing the owners ensconced in their private chambers. This provided more efficient circulation, greater privacy and helped distance the staff from the owners. The segregation of the classes began to be expressed in architecture.

Across the hills in the Severn valley stands Plasnewydd (Carno), a very similar building to Tyfaenor, but constructed a few generations later and with timber-framed walls. Here however, the building is two rooms deep and is basically two houses backing onto each other. The less important rooms (kitchen, dairy, servants' quarters) have been banished to the rear unit. This is an example of a *double-pile* plan, which achieved great popularity in the eighteenth century. With this type of house there were generally two roofs with a central valley, sometimes hidden behind raised parapets.

Figure G: a centrally-planned house

Another innovation of the period was the growing importance of the parlour, which began to replace the hall as the main room of the house. The hall might still retain a central location, but it would be more of an impressive vestibule containing the main stairs and circulation space, rather than the busy communal chamber of yore. Great House (Monmouth), built for Henry Somerset in 1673, shows this trend clearly; the restrained classical façade is divided into three equal parts, with the central recessed section containing the entry hall and stair. **Tredegar House** (Newport), built for William Morgan around 1670, has the same basic arrangement, albeit on a far grander scale and with a flourish of baroque ornamentation.

Great House, Monmouth

The exuberance of the early Renaissance gave way in around 1700 to a rather stiff and bland classicism that strove for architectural simplicity. Box-like houses with rows of tall sash windows became the norm and the vernacular tradition was slowly left behind. A typical example of this restrained style is Erddig (Wrexham), built in 1687 and refaced and extended in 1772. Llandaff Court (Cardiff), built by Thomas Matthews in the 1740s, has a very similar layout with three storeys of windows perfectly arranged around a central doorway. A more modest example of this type of house is Glandwr (Grosmont), which bears the date 1742 above the front entrance. For the average farmhouse the central stair-passage layout with a catslide roof (*Figure H*) proved to be the most popular design and this plan was built throughout the countryside up to the present day.

Figure H: a house with a central stair passage

Cottage industries and gothic fantasies

The close link between the craftsman and his materials was gradually lost in the early 1800s as builders used pattern-book designs to erect rows of terraced houses and characterless dwellings. The improving transport system also had a major effect, introducing mass-produced brick and slate into areas previously dominated by local building materials.

The lingering vernacular tradition was now represented by the humble cottage, those little dwellings built by the poorer members of society lacking sufficient land and money to afford a more substantial home. Many cottages were built as smallholdings on marginal land because the rural population increased during the latter part of the eighteenth century, putting pressure on available resources. An estimated half of the population was living in cottages and sought a livelihood working on farm estates or quarries. By the middle of the nineteenth century the situation stabilised as people moved away from the countryside and into the rapidly expanding industrial towns of Wales.

This roadside cottage at Llanddowror (Carmarthen) has been extended to the left and had its thatched roof replaced

Travellers in the uplands frequently encounter the abandoned ruins of tiny cottages and might wonder how anyone could have eked out a living in such a remote and bare landscape. A writer passing through the moors of north Pembrokeshire in 1899 was astonished to see over forty empty cottages. 'We must suppose that life is too hard, the rewards too slight, the inconveniences of isolation too manifest', wrote Sir Cyril Fox in 1937. Many of these smallholdings began life as a temporary *hafod*, occupied as first by shepherds during the summer months and then gradually taken over on a more permanent basis. This is suggested by the 1744 survey of the Manor of Perfedd in north Cardiganshire: 'Interspersed all over the Common there are small cottages which were originally summer houses for shepherds and have an inclosure of a few acres of ground annexed to them.'

Other cottages claim origin from an even more transient structure, a *ty unnos* ('one night house'), which was reputedly built between dusk and dawn in order to lay claim to the surrounding land. The materials used were turf blocks for the walls and thatch for the roof; and the boundaries of the surrounding land were determined by the distance the builder could throw an axe from the threshold. Modern attempts have proved that it is quite possible to erect a simple hut in one night, if all the materials are prepared beforehand and there are plenty of willing helpers. The legality of such squatter houses has often been brought into question, but many pioneers established a foothold in this way. Such is believed to be the origin of **Penrhos Cottage** (Maenclochog), although this substantial little building would

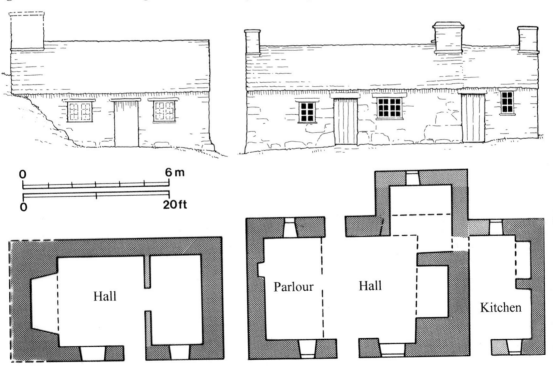

Plans and elevations of two north Wales cottages.
Left: Hafod-y-gelyn (Aber); right: Merbwll (Llanaelhearn)

Penrhos Cottage, Maenclochog

definitely take more than one night to complete! Clearly the first *ty unnos* would be a crude temporary structure swiftly replaced with more durable materials.

Cottages followed the same basic layout patterns as the middle-class houses of the period and were similarly built from whatever materials could be obtained locally. The most common type is a direct-entry dwelling with a central doorway; but in certain areas of the country diminutive examples of the hearth-passage and lobby-entry plans can be found. There is usually just one room inside, perhaps with a flimsy partition to divide off a smaller chamber variously used as a dairy, pantry, parlour or bedroom. In the case of **Llainfadyn**, a slate workers cottage of 1762 from Rhostryfan (now at St Fagans), the division was achieved by placing large cupboard-beds across the room. Rarely was there an upper floor in these little houses and the main chamber was open to the roof, rather like a miniature medieval hall. However, there might be a half-attic (*croglofft*) over the smaller room.

The lower down the social ladder you were, the poorer was your home. Because they tended to be built from perishable or poor-quality materials, the majority of cottages and squatter dwellings that survive today tend to be fairly late in date. In most cases the owner would have constructed it himself without resorting to a local builder. Brick, stone and timber-framing were commonly used, but the very poor had to make do with earth and mud. In rural parts of Cardiganshire and Carmarthenshire some of these humble dwellings still remain today (though heavily modernised) and a reconstructed example from **Nantwallter** can be seen at St Fagans. The floor is of beaten earth, the walls are built up from layers of dried mud and the shaggy thatched roof is supported on crudely jointed scarfed-crucks. A single fire burns at one end, with the smoke rising up through a wattle chimney.

A seventeenth-century lampoonist unflatteringly compared such crude turf houses to 'a great blot of cow-turd'. In 1847 squatter dwellings in mid Wales were described as presenting 'a wretched appearance, being often built of mud and wattling and thatched with rushes or heather … a tapering aperture in the roof serves for a chimney, but quite often as not the smoke escapes by the door … mellowing every article of furniture as well as the complexion of the inmates. Many … have their fires of peat … on the floor in the centre of the dwelling'. A few generations earlier in Caernarfonshire, a brave traveller entered another poor cottage. 'The dark mud wall, rocky floor, and few brown rushes [the family bed] suggested the idea of a den; the parents and their numerous progeny were assembled round a small peat fire.' It is worth quoting these accounts because they reveal that for the underclass of Welsh society, domestic comfort had not moved on since prehistoric times. Indeed, if a Neolithic or Iron Age farmer were transported to early nineteenth-century Wales he would no doubt feel quite at home in such a humble dwelling.

During the nineteenth century the rising population in the growing industrial towns demanded new housing on a vast scale. At first, the workers' houses had a nodding acquaintance with traditional architecture, in that they were semi-detached buildings

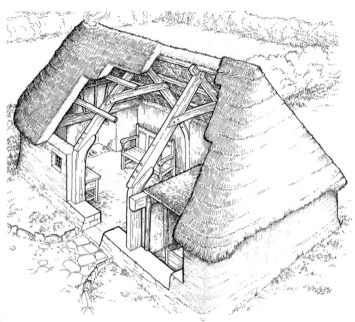

Cutaway drawing of a clay-walled cottage once at Nantwallter, now at St Fagans, showing the scarfed cruck construction

with exposed beamed ceilings and stone winding stairs next to the fireplace. However, they were built on a much smaller scale and more people were squeezed into the living space than before. If you want to see the kind of house your grandparents probably lived in, pay a visit to St Fagans, where the award-winning reconstructed terrace of six houses from Rhyd-y-car (Merthyr) shows the gamut of home comforts from 1805 to 1985.

Architects had barely adjusted to the aesthetic restrictions of the classical style when an exuberant theatricality exploded across the nineteenth century. An Englishman's (and Welshman's) home quite literally became his castle. What began as a light-hearted movement concerned with a few decorative effects rapidly escalated into the dominant architectural style of the century. The grand baronial mansions springing up in the course of the gothic revival could not have existed in any other century than the nineteenth. Architects immersed themselves in medieval architecture and the works of Sir Walter Scott, applied fiddly gothic details to over-large country houses and pretended they were ancient monuments. The make-believe whimsies of William Burges (Castell Coch) or Thomas Hopper (Penrhyn Castle) are palatable in small doses, but when almost every house had to have its pointed arch or fake timber-frame, the result could be repetitive and cloying.

There were still some builders who understood the simpler styles and techniques of traditional architecture and its place in the modern world, and now, after a gap of some two hundred years, the vernacular tradition is struggling to make a comeback. Imaginative

A modern house near Wrexham, built using traditional timber-frame methods

designers and homebuilders with enough capital can afford to experiment and break away from symmetry and order to create something individual. The open-plan multi-purpose living space of the medieval period has resurfaced from the closeted box-rooms of our Victorian heritage. The regimented terrace has been replaced with semi-detached dwellings that take pride in their building materials and are not hidden behind rendering or Cotswold stone cladding. New use for old buildings is on the agenda; Castell-y-fan, Cefn Mably and Sker House are just three examples of ruined Glamorgan mansions recently reconstructed and given new life as upmarket flats. And how much more traditional can you get than the Iron Age-style thatched round hut of Ty Crwn (St Hilary) or the timber-framed cruck hall of Ty'r Dderwen (Pontardawe)? – just two examples of modern houses successfully fusing ancient building techniques and materials with the complex needs of contemporary life.

Places to visit

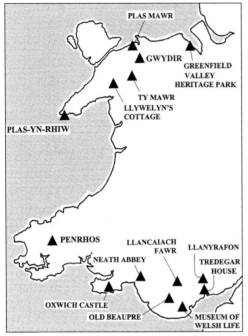

Aberdaron *Plas-yn-rhiw*

This National Trust-owned property overlooks the broad sweep of Porth Neigwl bay near the tip of the Lleyn peninsula. Although said to be medieval, the building probably dates from 1634 and underwent extensive renovations around 1820. It seems to have been a typical regional house of direct-entry plan, with a stone winding stair beside the massive gable fireplace. In 1937 the derelict house was purchased by the Keating sisters and only through their care and dedication was the property saved for posterity.

Access: Plas-yn-rhiw lies midway between Aberdaron and Abersoch on the Lleyn peninsula. Turn off the B44413 at Botwnnog and follow the signs to Rhiw. The way to the house is signposted from the village. It is open daily except Tuesday, 12-5 from April to October (OS map ref: SH 237 283).

Beddgelert *'Llywelyn's Cottage'*

This attractive stone house has nothing whatsoever to do with the Welsh prince Llywelyn, nor with the spurious nonsense linking his fictional dog 'Gelert' to this little village nestling in the shadow of Eryri. Originally it was known as Ty-isaf ('lower house') and was far too substantial to be a cottage in the true sense of the word. Clearly this was the residence of a moderately wealthy landowner rather than a poor labourer. It is a typical example of a regional direct-entry house, probably dating from the late sixteenth century with later alterations (most notably the heightening of the roof – in the attic you can see the massive original trusses playing piggyback with the later ones). Just inside the entrance there is the remains of an oak post-and-panel screen that originally divided the interior into two unequally sized rooms. The outer room now contains displays and information about the locality, while the hall with its massive gable fireplace is now a National Trust gift shop.

Access: The National Trust owns the house and the ground-floor rooms are freely accessible daily 11-5, March-October. It lies next to the bridge in the centre of Beddgelert village, south-east of Caernarfon on the A4085 to Porthmadog (OS map ref: SH 590 481).

Conwy *Plas Mawr*

After painstaking renovation work lasting some four years and costing two million pounds, this sixteenth-century building now ranks as one of the best-preserved Elizabethan town houses in Britain. The crumbling stonework has been renewed and the bare walls treated to a gleaming coat of limewash; the rooms have been redecorated and furnished in such authentic detail that you might expect the original owners to walk in at any moment. Indeed, the vibrant colour scheme and richly decorated wall hangings may come as a surprise to many visitors familiar with the rather stark Victorian image of 'Tudorbethan' decor. All the principal rooms have extensive plasterwork on the walls and ceilings, highlighting the Elizabethan fashion for heraldic ornamentation and ostentatious display.

Plas Mawr was built by a wealthy merchant, Robert Wynn (1520-1598), soon after his marriage to Dorothy Griffith. His family home was at **Gwydyr** further up the Conwy valley and though certain features of traditional local architecture appear at Plas Mawr, there is a stronger influence from further afield. Robert had travelled abroad in the service of the court diplomat Sir Philip Hoby and would no doubt have seen the different styles of architecture prevalent on the Continent. His contemporary, Sir Richard Clough, had introduced the distinctive Flemish style crow-stepped gable into Wales and now Robert used the same detail on his new house.

The house was built in three main stages as Robert bought up the neighbouring tenements in the centre of the medieval walled town. First to go up was the north wing, with

Plas Mawr (see also p.86)

its very advanced plan of two chambers separated by a central entrance lobby and service room. This was completed in 1577 and over the next two years the main part of the house was built, resulting in an ambitious H-plan residence. The central section is taken up with a ground floor kitchen and pantry, with a single large chamber above. It is clear that this upper chamber was originally intended to serve as a first-floor hall with an ornate arch-braced roof (like the one still to be seen at Gwydyr), but Robert changed his mind during the course of construction and substituted a more contemporary flat plaster ceiling. The great oak trusses can now only be seen from the attic.

The south wing is almost a mirror image of its northern counterpart, although a large and imposing hall takes up much of the ground-floor space. Despite the presence of an archaic hall, Robert was no slavish follower of tradition; access was through a rather insignificant doorway from the courtyard, first passing a large stair spiralling up to the more important private chambers on the upper floors. Only when Robert acquired the plot fronting High Street and built a substantial gatehouse was the principal entry to the house redirected through this room. Clearly the former significance of the hall had diminished by the Elizabethan period.

Building work had virtually finished by 1590 and only minor alterations were carried out over the succeeding centuries, as the house was adapted to changing needs. By the end of the seventeenth century it was no longer the main family residence and was rented out. The gatehouse was used as a court, the main building divided up into tenements, and in the nineteenth century part was used as an infant school. Towards the end of the century Plas Mawr was taken over by the Royal Cambrian Academy of Art, before ownership passed to CADW in 1993 and a lengthy programme of restoration work began.

Access: In the care of CADW and open daily (except Mon) 9.30-5, April to October. Plas Mawr lies in the heart of the fortified town of Conwy, off the A55 near Llandudno (OS map ref: 780 775).

Cowbridge *Old Beaupre*

Beaupre was one of the finest Elizabethan manor houses in the fertile Vale of Glamorgan, an area of the country particularly rich in such grand edifices. Now it is an echoing shell, devoid of floors and roof, one wing alone still occupied. The Basset family acquired the manor in the fourteenth century and for the next three centuries they built, extended and embellished, until a series of crippling financial problems led to the neglect and eventual sale of the estate in 1709. Thereafter the greater part of the building was left to rot.

Much of the surviving masonry dates from the early fourteenth century and forms a group of detached stone buildings arranged around a central courtyard, including a two-storey hall block and a kitchen wing (now the inhabited farmhouse). Although it is still marked on maps as a 'castle' Beaupre was never fortified, although there are hints of defensive considerations in the gatehouse and tower block adjoining the hall. What gave rise to this

Old Beaupre (also see photograph on p.88)

tradition was the Elizabethan hankering after make-believe feudalism. Between 1540 and 1600 the manor was remodelled and extended around a new north-facing courtyard, which was provided with battlemented walls and an outer gatehouse. Set above the Renaissance archway is a heraldic plaque dated 1586 and bearing the initials of Richard Basset and his first wife Catherine. The classical details sit rather uncomfortably with the pseudo-gothic features, but this didn't stop Richard from going even further and adding a splendidly incongruous porch to the hall. This 'Tower of the Orders' (so called because it displays columns of Doric, Ionic and Corinthian Orders) was probably carved in Somerset and imported at Richard's request, although the origin for the design is French. Among the lavish details is an inscription bearing the date 1600 and the name of his *third* wife – clearly Richard had led a busy marital life in the intervening years!

The great hall is largely a medieval structure and the Elizabethan alterations entailed a new fireplace and spacious windows. Though the bare walls are now devoid of the decorative plaster that once adorned them, it is at least possible to make out the blocked-up doors and windows of the earlier phase. The upper floors were reached from a typically grand Elizabethan staircase, but previously the lords of Beaupre had to make do with the dark and cramped stair-passages tunnelling through the thick walls. The Basset family were not the only members of the local aristocracy to plough the profits of their lands into stone and mortar. The Mansels of **Oxwich**, the Aubreys of Llantrithyd, the Morgans of Rhiwperra and the Turbevilles of Sker all did the same, raising huge and costly buildings that proved too unwieldy for use in later years.

Access: The ruined part of Old Beaupre is in the care of CADW and freely accessible. The house lies south-east of Cowbridge off the A48. Follow signs to St Athan and after about 2km there is a small parking area opposite Howe Mill house. From here a signposted footpath crosses the fields to the house (OS map ref: ST 009 720).

Cwmbran *Llanyrafon Farm Museum*
This is one of the few old houses to survive the birth of modern-day Cwmbran in the 1970s. No one knows who built the original house here in the late sixteenth century, but it was a modest dwelling, typical of the hill farms of the region, with a hearth-passage hall and two inner rooms behind a post-and-panel screen. A fragmentary cruck embedded in the rear wall indicates that there was a timber-framed predecessor on the same site. In the early seventeenth century the Griffiths family enlarged the house in the up-to-date Renaissance style by adding a three-storey block with a tall porch and rear stair wing, completely dwarfing the older farmstead. Within the lofty new hall there was a wooden screen and a finely carved stone lateral fireplace. Later members of the family considerably extended Llanyrafon, but when the line died out in the late nineteenth century the grand house became a tenanted farm and slowly fell into decay. Restoration work has started, but it will be some years before the building is fully opened to the public.

Access: Llanyrafon is owned by the Torfaen Museum Trust and is usually open for tours in the summer, but at the time of writing is closed for renovation work. The house can be seen from the roadside east of Cwmbran town centre, off the A4042, M4 junction 25a (OS map ref: ST 303 946).

Gelligaer *Llancaiach Fawr*

Upland Glamorgan in the early sixteenth century was a far from safe and tranquil landscape; vagabonds roamed the hills, thieves lurked in the dense woodlands to pick off unwary travellers, and violent quarrels frequently broke out amongst neighbouring landowners. It comes as no surprise to find that when Richard ap Lewis (or his son David) began constructing Llancaiach Fawr, defensive considerations played a major role in the design. The only entrance was secured by a stout drawbar and the ground-floor windows are small and heavily barred to prevent unwarranted access. A little turret contains privies on two levels – just the thing if you couldn't get outside to answer the call of nature. Even more remarkably, the house has narrow stone stairs built into the thick walls, closely resembling the dark passageways found in local castles.

Apart from these unusual details, the house was built to the traditional three-unit plan with a storeyed porch at the front and a rear wing containing an additional suite of private rooms. All the principal chambers are on the first floor, including a spacious hall with a lateral fireplace and a plaster ceiling that would no doubt originally have been richly decorated. A connecting doorway leads through to the parlour (which could be closed off from the rest of the house if occasion demanded). All the walls here are lined with dark wood panelling put up around 1630, but they would originally have been plastered and perhaps painted, with decorative wall hangings and tapestries.

Llancaiach Fawr

By the seventeenth century the family had adopted the surname Pritchard, and Edward Pritchard carried out alterations to the house, most notably the addition of a large stair to create a more prestigious approach to the hall. Edward entertained the beleaguered King Charles I here in the summer of 1645, but his Puritan sympathies led him to side with the Parliamentarian cause. 'Colonel' Pritchard (as he was known) successfully defended Cardiff Castle against a Royalist attack the following year and was later commended for his action. This was the high point in the family fortunes. Llancaiach later passed through various hands until the local council acquired it in 1981 and began a lengthy process of restoration work. Rather than simply open the house as a static museum piece a more imaginative approach was adopted; the interior has been furnished as it would have been in the 1640s and costumed staff show visitors around the house and explain various aspects of daily life in Colonel Pritchard's time. There is a modern museum building close

Cutaway reconstruction of Llancaiach Fawr as it looked around 1550. The unusual layout with multiple doors and mural stairs can be appreciated in this view

by, where the house and its history is explored in detail, and various events are held in the grounds at certain times of the year.

Access: Llancaiach Fawr is owned by Caerphilly County Council and is open daily 10-5 for most of the year (closed Mondays November to February). The house lies next to the B4254 between Nelson and Gelligaer, and there are ample signs pointing the way from either the A470 Cardiff to Merthyr road (M4 junction 32) or the A469 from Caerphilly (OS map ref ST 114 967).

Gower *Oxwich Castle*

Oxwich is a castle in name only, for whatever medieval building stood here was swallowed up in a huge Tudor mansion built by the Mansel family in the sixteenth century. Its military ancestry is reflected in the courtyard wall studded with turrets and battlements; but all this was meant to impress visitors, not repel invaders. Over the gateway is a stone plaque bearing the arms of Sir Rice Mansel, who began rebuilding his family home around 1520. His son Edward continued the work, creating an early (and very ambitious) example of the great 'prodigy houses' that sprang up across Britain in the Elizabethan age. All is now in ruin, for the Mansels soon abandoned Oxwich to the tender mercies of tenant farmers. By

Oxwich Castle

the nineteenth century only one wing was inhabited and the crumbling building was even threatened with demolition as late as 1949, before being placed in State Guardianship.

Oxwich is impressive even in ruin, a huge three-storey block with cliff-like walls pierced with gaping window openings. Unfortunately much has gone and we are now left with the stark shell of a building devoid of roof, woodwork, panelling, tapestries, glazed windows and plastered ceilings. The main part is an enormous block containing vaulted stores on the ground floor and a huge first-floor hall crowned by a long gallery running the length of the building. Three turrets jut out from the back forming an E-shaped plan. The most complete turret is a remarkable six storeys high with numerous residential chambers for guests and retainers. Two huge staircases at either end of the building provided access to all levels. The much smaller south wing is still roofed, for it was used as a farmhouse long after the rest of this leviathan fell into decay.

Access: The house is in the care of CADW and is open 10-5 April to September. The castle lies on the hillside above Oxwich village on the Gower Peninsula, about 16km west of Swansea (M4 junction 42). Follow the signs from the city centre to Gower and Port Eynon via the A4118 (OS map ref: SS 498 863).

Holywell *Greenfield Valley Heritage Centre*

One end of the Greenfield valley is crowned by the famous holy well of St Gwenfrewi, while at the opposite end the forlorn ruins of Basingwerk Abbey slumber beside the Dee estuary. The powerful stream born from the well was used to turn the wheels of the various mills and factories established along the valley. Now the industrial, agricultural and religious heritage of the area is commemorated in the visitor centre and museum of buildings lying within the shadow of the abbey. Among the buildings open to the public is a re-erected farmhouse brought here in the 1980s from the village of Lixwm a few miles away.

Pentre Farm had been empty and derelict for many years and it was only during survey work that the complex history of this stone long-house was unravelled. We know from records that the Kenrick family owned the house in 1660s, but by then it was already a hundred years old, having started life as a simple hall divided into a living area and cowshed. Around 1600 a fireplace and chimney was built to replace the open hearth and a loft space put in over the inner room. A few generations later, the low roof was raised over the dwelling end creating a full upper floor and a rather grand stair turret was added to the front façade. In subsequent years Pentre Farm underwent further changes, including the conversion of the cowshed into a parlour. When the building was moved to Greenfield it was decided to recreate it as it was in the time of the Kenricks, just after the stair and upper floor had been added, but before the cowshed was altered. The house has now been stocked with antique furniture, giving a good impression of a seventeenth-century interior.

Pentre Farm, Greenfield Valley Heritage Centre

Access: The Heritage Park is open daily 10-4.30 April to October and lies on the B5121 close to Greenfield, just off the A548 coast road between Flint and Rhyl (OS map ref: SJ 197 774).

Llanrwst *Gwydyr Castle*

When Maredudd ap Ieuan decided to move home in 1488, he repaired and reoccupied the old Welsh mountain stronghold of Dolwyddelan Castle. After some years spent acquiring more properties and consolidating gains, he relocated to Llanrwst and built for himself a more comfortable version of the grim castle keep. It is a self-contained block with privies, fireplaces, spiral stairs and accommodation on four floors; a sort of castle in looks, if not in reality. There are no battlements and the only protection against attack was a thick wooden door secured by a drawbar. When Maredudd died in 1525 he had established his seat here at Gwydyr and laid the foundations for one of the most important families in north Wales.

His son John (d.1559) adopted the surname Wynn and continued with the building work, using medieval stones taken from the recently closed abbey of Maenan nearby. Further work was carried out by his son, the historian Sir John Wynn (1553–1627), and later generations of the family extended, altered and rebuilt according to their tastes. William Morgan of **Ty Mawr** was educated at Gwydyr and from here Robert Wynn left to seek a career at court, returning to build the more stunning edifice of **Plas Mawr** in 1576. Even the

Gwydyr Castle

105

famous court architect Inigo Jones is said to have stayed at Gwydyr and reputedly designed the humpbacked bridge into Llanrwst. Over the years the house has grown into its present sprawling layout and many gothic features (along with the 'castle' misnomer) are due to enthusiastic Victorian restorations. Gwydyr is slowly being restored after two destructive fires in the twentieth century.

The long low range adjoining Maredudd's tower was added by his son John around 1550, not as a traditional hall-house, but as one of the new storeyed houses appearing throughout the country. On the ground floor there is a large hall with a massive beamed ceiling, entered along a cross-passage at its lower end. Beyond a post-and-panel screen at one side of the passage stood two service rooms. At the opposite end of the hall there is a huge stone fireplace, but this is not an original feature because it has been built behind a timber-framed partition rising the full height of the house. This appears to be an early type of chimney known as a *smoke-bay*, which was designed to channel away fumes from an open fire. A splendid chamber roofed over with arch-braced trusses occupies all of the first floor. This seems too large to have been a private room or parlour and may have had a more public function. Perhaps this was the main dining hall for the Wynns and their guests and its design may well have inspired Robert to build something very similar at Plas Mawr.

Access: Gwydyr Castle is open daily 10-4 March to October (except Mondays and Saturdays) and lies just west of Llanrwst in the Conwy valley, on the B5106 to Betws-y-coed (OS map ref: SH 796 610). A charming little seventeenth-century chapel is also open to the public and lies in the woods above the house.

Maenclochog *Penrhos Cottage*

Penrhos stands on the edge of the Preseli Mountains, an area of bleak moorlands and craggy peaks, dotted with lonely farmsteads and prehistoric relics. This too is a monument of a sort, to the poor farmers forced to colonise the fringes of agricultural land in the eighteenth century. It was widely believed that a person could gain freehold rights to a plot of common land if a house could be built on it in a single night. Penrhos, like many other smallholdings, traces its origin from such huts but small though it is, it would have taken a lot longer than one night to build it. Within the whitewashed thatched cottage there is just a single low room with a small fireplace in the end wall, and a loft above. A small bedroom extension was built around 1840. Originally the house was built by the Williams family in the early-nineteenth century, and was last occupied in the 1960s. (See photograph on p.94)

Access: The cottage is owned by Pembrokeshire County Council and is usually open on Mondays 11-4 in July-Aug. Maenclochog lies on the B4313 between Narberth and Fishguard in west Wales. Head out of the village towards Mynachlog-ddu and take the first right over the bridge to Llangolman. After about 1.5km there is a right turn to Llanycefn; follow this for about 2km and the cottage will be found by the roadside at the top of the hill (OS map ref: SN 102 258).

Neath *Neath Abbey*

Gaunt fragments alone remain of this site, but the sheer scale of the ruins reveals the wealth and ambition of its Elizabethan owner. Neath was one of the grandest monastic houses in Wales, but in 1540 the estate was seized by the Crown and sold off to Sir Richard Williams. One of the last abbots had already set about converting part of the monastery buildings into a private residence and Richard (or his son Henry) just completed the task. Only the outer walls of the house now survive, but enough remains to identify it as a typical Elizabethan mansion with rows of square windows, tall chimneys and clusters of dormers along the roofline. The plan was restricted by the older buildings and formed a sort of H-shaped arrangement of two long wings connected by shorter blocks. There was a large hall with a lateral chimney and, adjoining it at one end, a long gallery extending for almost 30m across the width of the building.

Access: In the care of CADW and open standard hours. Neath Abbey lies just 1km west of Neath town centre, off the A4230 to Skewen, M4 junction 43 (OS map ref: SS 737 974).

Newport *Tredegar House*

Great stately homes like Tredegar, Bodrhyddan (Rhyl) and Erddig (Wrexham) are really outside the scope of a book principally concerned with traditional domestic architecture. They were built by professional architects to designs and layouts from pattern books, rather than by local craftsmen using techniques and skills inherited over the generations. Tredegar finds a place here as a representative of this class of building, for not only has it changed little over the three hundred years since it was built, but the existing baroque mansion also incorporates the medieval house of the Morgan family.

Tredegar House, Newport. The older medieval hall can be seen on the right

The Morgans were among the greatest and most widespread of Welsh families, and their rise to power was given a boost when Sir John Morgan supported Henry Tudor at Bosworth in 1485. When the dust of battle settled and the new Tudor king had duly rewarded his followers, the Morgans built a new house at Tredegar, which the court historian, John Leland, described as 'a very fair place of stone' in about 1540. Only one wing of this house survives, easily distinguished from the later works by the plain stone walls and chunky lateral chimneys. The large arched windows of the hall look inwards toward the courtyard in a typical medieval fashion, but when Sir William Morgan began to redesign the house in the 1660s his new buildings looked *outwards*, across the extensive parklands and landscaped gardens to the Monmouthshire hills. The modest grey walls were replaced by a grandiose brick mansion two storeys high, with attic rooms under a high-pitched roof crowned with a balustraded walkway. The warm brickwork is enlivened with ornamental features and heraldic beasts carved from Bath stone. Great expanses of glass brightened up the interior rooms with their lavish panelling, gilded walls and painted ceilings. No wonder that the famous court architect, Inigo Jones, was once believed (wrongly) to have been the architect of this exuberant house.

Despite the late date, the interior layout reflects the archaic arrangement of a medieval house, where rooms are set in a line opening off each other. Sir William managed to build two wings of his house before he died in 1680, and it seems the full plan of a square building with a central courtyard was never realised. There were further additions, but after 1900 the family fortunes dwindled and crippling death duties led to the sale of the estate in 1951. The grand mansion was used as a school until the local council acquired the run-down property in 1974 and began a lengthy process of renovations and repairs. Tredegar House is now justly reckoned to be the finest stately home in Wales and one of the most impressive examples of Restoration architecture in Britain.

Access: Tredegar House lies west of Newport, just off M4 junction 28. It is run by Newport County Borough Council and guided tours are available Easter-October, Wed-Sun 11.30-4 (OS map ref: ST 288 853).

St Fagans *The National History Museum*
'A folk museum represents the life and culture of a nation, illustrating the arts and crafts and in particular the building crafts, of the complete community', wrote Iorwerth Peate, the first curator of St Fagans Museum and author of *The Welsh House*. This is one of the largest open-air museums in Europe and has the most varied and extensive collection of buildings in Britain. Over forty from various parts of Wales have been rebuilt here and furnished to represent an aspect of the region and society to which they once belonged. The museum buildings not only show the various construction techniques and materials used over the centuries (earth, brick, stone, timber), but also range in date from the ancient (a reconstructed Celtic village) to the modern (a 1940s prefab). The collection was established in 1946 by the National Museum of Wales within the grounds of St Fagans Castle. Apart from the re-

St Fagans

erected buildings there is also a modern gallery housing an extensive collection of artefacts highlighting the cultural heritage of Wales, including historical costumes, artworks, musical instruments and household goods. Visitors can also explore some buildings that provide an insight into the agricultural background of the houses, such as a sixteenth-century cruck barn, a slate-built hayshed, and a remarkable beehive-shaped pigsty.

Long before the museum was ever conceived of, **St Fagans Castle** stood guard over the little village and church. The De la Sor family established a stronghold here in the Middle Ages, but by 1500 it had fallen into decay. A wealthy local lawyer, Dr John Gibbon, purchased the estate and was probably responsible for building the existing house within the ruined walls of the castle around 1580. In 1586 he sold the estate to his brother-in-law, Nicholas Herbert. In 1616 Edward Lewis of Caerphilly acquired the property and it remained with this family until donated to the museum. For much of this time the Lewis family neglected St Fagans in favour of their English estates and by the nineteenth century it was used as the village school. Soon after 1850 St Fagans was reoccupied as the residence of Robert Windsor-Clive (the family heir) and the building was extensively refurbished and stocked with antique furnishings of various periods brought from other houses. The interior has since been restored to its late nineteenth-century appearance.

When seen from above the house is shaped like a capital E, consisting of a central block with a storeyed porch, and two short wings projecting forward at each end. According to tradition, this type of house is supposed to have been inspired by the first initial of Queen Elizabeth's name. The façade is a perfect example of Renaissance symmetry, with rows of mullioned windows and dormers lighting the attic level. The interior, however, still owes much to traditional building plans. There is a large hall, a kitchen and service room at the lower end and a parlour or dining room at the upper. The centrally placed porch opens directly into the hall, where a cross-passage leads through to a long rear corridor running the length of the house. From this corridor most of the rooms are accessed, but in order to conform to the E-plan it was necessary to squeeze the stairs into the furthest corners, which made for less effective circulation. On the first floor the rear corridor functioned as a long gallery, a *de rigueur* feature of Elizabethan great houses, where the gentry might perambulate and enjoy the tapestries, paintings and vistas on rainy days.

Abernodwydd

Abernodwydd is undoubtedly the most photogenic of the museum buildings, a splendid little timber-framed thatched house brought here from Llangadfan in mid Wales. As originally built, Abernodwydd had the usual three-unit plan of an outer room, hall, and inner rooms in line, the sections being divided by box-framed partitions. The central hall was open to the roof, while the two end units had upper floors reached by ladders. We have already encountered this plan in the medieval period, but what is most surprising about this house is the date it was built. Recent analysis of the timber beams established that it was constructed in 1678, which is remarkably late for an open hall. Documents record the owner of the house at that time as Rhys Evan. His son put an upper floor over the hall in 1708 and replaced the open hearth with a fireplace and chimney, creating a lobby-entry plan. Even with these modifications, only the back wall of the fireplace was built from stone – the flue is timber-framed and the sides of the hearth are enclosed by wooden panels with built-in benches. The fire hazards of such a structure were demonstrated a few years ago when a spark from the smouldering hearth ignited the thatch. Though the roof was badly damaged, most of the oak framing and antique furniture was saved, and Abernodwydd was carefully restored to its former condition.

Cilewent was brought from the bleak hills above Rhayader, where the original long-house was under threat from the rising waters of the Claerwen reservoir. This was originally a late fifteenth-century timber-framed hall, but in 1734 (the date is carved over the front door) the walls were completely rebuilt in stone. In its eighteenth-century incarnation, Cilewent contains a stable and cowshed at the lower end and a single dwelling chamber at the upper. A timber partition separates the two halves, in complete contrast to most

Cilewent

long-houses of the period, where the main fireplace acts as the divider. Here the hall has a cavernous fireplace in the end gable wall. Behind a timber-framed partition in the rear wall is a dairy wing with another gable fireplace. From the hall a stair beside the fireplace climbs to the dimly lit sleeping chambers in the attic.

Garreg Fawr was originally built in 1544 and epitomises the small, solid houses of direct-entry plan found in the mountainous areas of north Wales. The exterior is stark and uninviting, with massively thick slate walls pierced by tiny windows; but inside the grim masonry is mellowed by the liberal use of carved oak and lime plaster. A post-and-panel screen separates two service rooms from the larger hall with its heavy beamed ceiling and cavernous gable fireplace. Most houses of this type have a stone winding stair in the corner beside the fireplace, but here there is only a precarious ladder leading up to the first floor. This might imply that the upper rooms were less important, but surprisingly there is a fairly plush residential chamber here with its own fireplace and ornate roof truss. The remaining space is taken up with a small bedchamber and a loft above.

Garreg Fawr

Hendre'r-ywydd Uchaf is the oldest building on display at the museum and recent analysis of the timbers pinpoint a construction date of 1508. This hall-house once stood in Llangynhafal in the Vale of Clwyd and at the time it was acquired by the museum in 1953, the exterior had been modernised to such an extent that hardly any evidence of its age was visible. The timbered walls were rendered over, stone chimneys replaced the open hearth; even the thatched roof was hidden under corrugated metal sheets. At St Fagans the house was reconstructed as a typical 'black and white' building, but in recent years opinion has changed as to how timber buildings originally looked and now all the exterior walls have been whitewashed. Hendre'r-ywydd is a small and simple type of medieval dwelling, containing a cowshed, outer room, hall and inner room in line. Each section is demarcated by a cruck-framed partition, while the end walls are box-framed. Unlike the grander hall-houses of the period, such as **Penarth Fawr** and **Ty Mawr**, there is no decorative truss spanning the main room here. The interior has been restored to its medieval appearance, with earthen floors, a sooty hearth and draughty unglazed windows.

Kennixton was the first house re-erected at St Fagans and was opened to the public in 1953. It was brought from Llangennith at the western end of the Gower Peninsula and shows features characteristic of that region. What looks like a large cupboard in the kitchen is in fact a box-bedstead (many Gower houses have this type of bed in an alcove projecting from the side wall). The 'charnel box' in the ceiling above the fireplace was used to hang and cure meat. Kennixton

Kennixton

is a typical end-entry hearth-passage house and was built in 1610. Originally this was a 'one-up-one-down' house with only a fireplace on the ground floor, but around 1680 the kitchen was added as an outer room. The older part has an unusual decorative scissor-tie roof truss and the thatched covering has been lined with intricately woven straw mats. In the eighteenth century the house was refurbished and a second kitchen wing added at right angles to the main block. The interior has now been furnished in the style of the 1790s, when Kennixton was home to the Rogers family.

The buildings described above were the homes of fairly prosperous farmers; the dwellings of the less well-off members of society are represented at St Fagans by two reconstructed cottages. *Llainfadyn* was the family home of a labourer who worked in the great slate quarries of north Wales. The interior has been furnished to represent the 1870s, although the house itself was built over a century earlier in 1762 (the date is carved into the crooked beam over the fireplace). Many of the rough boulders used to build the cottage are so massive that they project right through the walls. There is only a single chamber inside, but two box-bedsteads placed side by side served to divide the interior. By placing boards over the tops of the beds a sort of half-attic (known as a *croglofft*) was achieved. This loft was reached by a ladder and would have been used as storage space or for a child's bedroom.

Nantwallter

Nantwallter (see also the cutaway drawing on p.95) from west Wales was built around the same time as Llainfadyn, but differs markedly in construction. It was the home of a labouring family even further down the social scale, as suggested by the spartan interior and basic furniture. Again, this is basically a one-room house, with a wattled partition dividing off an outer chamber with a *croglofft* above. The walls are built of clom (a mix of clay, small stones and straw) with a thatched roof held up by timbers pegged together to form rough crucks. As with timber-framed buildings, it was necessary to build a stone plinth to prevent the damp ground from decaying the walls. On this foundation the walls were built up, each layer allowed to dry for several days before the next could be added to avoid slumping. The completed walls were smoothed down, door and window openings cut square and a protective coat of limewash applied. The dark and smoky interior with its bare earth floor clearly shows the level of comfort enjoyed by the humble occupants of this cottage.

In fact, comparison with the nearby **Celtic Village** shows that for some, very little had changed in their domestic environment since the Iron Age. Three round houses have been reconstructed here, based on evidence gathered from various archaeological excavations. Certain details are of course conjectural, because only slight foundations or a pattern of postholes ever survive of these buildings, but the houses still give a vivid impression of home comforts two thousand years ago. Most of the smoke from the central hearth rises to the high pointed thatched roof, so the atmosphere is not as noxious as you might think, for there is plenty of draught from the open doors and the central fire provides all-round heat. Scattered about the floor are plain wooden benches and seats, simple looms for weaving and stone hand-mills for grinding corn. The largest house has its roof supported on a ring of upright timbers, which have been used to form partitioned sleeping chambers around the outer walls. Even our distant ancestors desired a modicum of privacy.

Access: St Fagans Museum is open all year from 10 till 5 and lies about 6km west of Cardiff. It can be reached by several roads from the city centre, and is clearly signposted from M4 junction 33 (OS map ref: ST 118 772).

Wybrnant *Ty Mawr*

Ty Mawr, Wybrnant

You would be forgiven for thinking Wybrnant the most remote place in Wales. From Penmachno village a narrow road climbs the wooded mountainside and crosses the moors, before descending steeply to a little valley where a handful of grey stone buildings huddle together. Ty Mawr is the oldest one here and, as its name ('great house') suggests, it was the most important. Although it may seem small and rather basic to modern eyes, it was a substantial dwelling for its time and place and it is sobering to realise that in 1841 ten people were living in it. Since 1951 the house has been in the care of the National Trust and has been restored as near as possible to its original condition. Contemporary features and fittings have been removed, the steeply sloping floor re-laid with stone slabs, old timbers exposed and modern windows replaced with traditional unglazed wooden frames. Antique furnishings add to the vivid impression of a typical middle-class house of the 1600s.

This restoration work was carried out in 1988 to celebrate the fourth centenary of the publication of Bishop Morgan's Welsh translation of the Bible. William Morgan was born here in 1545 – not in the fine stone house that now survives, but in a small timber hall-house on the same site. Fragments of two crucks have been discovered embedded in the walls and these would have formed part of the early structure. Morgan left Wales in 1565 for a career in the church, becoming Bishop of Llandaff and then of St Asaph. By the time of his death in 1607, the owners of Ty Mawr had rebuilt their hall-house in stone, added a loft and replaced the open hearth with a large fireplace in the end wall. The upper floor contains a single long room with three hefty oak trusses and a gable fireplace. Here you can see several early Bibles and prayer books, including a copy of William's 1588 edition. The ground floor has undergone many alterations over the years and the present layout is a rather conjectural restoration. There is a long narrow hall, a central entrance lobby and two outer rooms, all separated by post-and-panel partitions. The concept of a central lobby providing access to the main rooms can be seen on a more ambitious scale at **Plas Mawr** (Conwy) and in a short time this type of plan would be refined even further by placing the main stair within the circulation space. If this was the original layout of Ty Mawr, it shows that the Renaissance ideals of symmetry and efficient circulation had reached even these remote corners of the country.

Access: The house is in the care of the National Trust and is open Thurs-Sun, 12-5, April-Oct. It lies a few kilometres south-west of Betws-y-Coed off the A5. Head towards Penmachno along the B4406, then follow the signs through the village and up over the mountain (OS map ref: SH 770 524).

Houses with limited public access

Aside from the buildings listed above which are generally accessible most (or part) of the year, there are a few houses that can be visited by appointment with the owner or which are open on special occasions (such as the European Heritage Days – see www.civictrustwales. org for further details). Furthermore, a number of historic buildings have been restored with grant aid from CADW and the owners must allow a certain amount of public access every year. A current list of these 'limited access houses' can be obtained from the CADW website.

The hammer-beam roof at Cochwillan

Bangor *Cochwillan*
One of the grandest hall-houses in Wales, Cochwillan was the home of William ap Gruffudd, High Sheriff of Caernarfonshire, one of many Welshmen who rose to power by supporting Henry Tudor's bid for the throne in 1485. The house was probably built soon after, to a traditional three-unit plan comprising a pair of outer rooms, central hall and private inner rooms. The great glory of this house is the hall roof, which has finely carved trusses supported on sturdy hammer-beams. Both ends of the house were altered in later years, before the whole was ignominiously downgraded to a barn (which at least prevented further modernisation). Conservation work has since restored this noble house to its original appearance. Open by appointment only, exterior visible from a public footpath (*OS map ref: SH 606 694*).

Talley *Aberdeunant*
This is a classic example of a Carmarthenshire scarfed-cruck house, recently restored by the National Trust. The colour-washed walls and thatched roof were formerly a common sight in this part of Wales. Aberdeunant belongs to the unit system group for there are actually two separate houses here (both of direct-entry plan), although one is no longer

occupied. The latter has been dendro-dated to 1793-96. The main house is probably not much older, although the thick, irregular walls may incorporate some early material and one of the roof timbers is an arch-braced cruck. All the others are scarfed-crucks formed of separate lengths of wood pegged together at the elbow, another common feature of this region. This is still a working farm and the interior has been left much as it was in the nineteenth century, with floral wallpaper and whitewashed beams (perhaps not everyone's idea of what an old house should look like!) There are guided tours of Aberdeunant on the first Saturday and Sunday of the month between May and September (*OS map ref: SN 672 308*).

Welshpool *Trewern Hall*
This has been described as one of the most outstanding timber-framed houses in Wales and indeed it is spectacular. Some of the walls have been replaced with stone and brick, but the lavishly decorated front façade is little altered from the time it was built in 1610. The principal feature of the house is a large ground-floor hall with a lateral chimney and bay windows to either side of the dais. Recent conservation work and analysis of the timber details suggest there was a late medieval house here, of which the kitchen, with its lower roofline and plainer walls, is the only remaining part. Open by appointment only (*OS map ref: SJ 268 114*).

Historic Pubs and Inns

The vast majority of early pubs in Wales started life as farms and houses used as meeting and drinking places by the locals. As tourists were drawn here in increasing numbers during the nineteenth century, more houses were turned over for commercial use and larger buildings were established to cater for their needs. Today, however, many small rural pubs struggle to survive. Some have been closed or converted back into houses, while others have been transformed into trendy bars. For further information on the subject I would direct the reader to my book *Historic Inns and Taverns of Wales and the Marches*. The following list is a selection of the most interesting buildings, retaining many original features and worth a visit.

Aberthaw *The Blue Anchor*

The Blue Anchor, Aberthaw

This is one of the few buildings in the Vale of Glamorgan retaining a once-commonplace thatched roof. The interior is a warren of dark stone rooms with low-beamed ceilings. The oldest part was built *c.*1550 as a hearth-passage house, with a kitchen subsequently added to the upper end. Interesting details include the wooden door to the inner room, ammonite fossils in the fireplace and narrow stone stairs built in straight flights within the thick walls *(OS map ref: ST 036 666)*.

Beaumaris *The George & Dragon*

Behind the nondescript rendered exterior is a superb timber-framed building dating from the mid sixteenth century (see the drawing on p.80). The ground floor was divided up into small rooms or shops, while the residential first floor had an unusual external gallery (like Tretower Court) overlooking the rear courtyard. However, the real gem of this building is the end chamber with its arch-braced roof and lavish wall paintings dating from 1610 *(OS map ref: 604 760)*.

Caerleon *The Old Bull Inn*

Originally built in the early sixteenth century as an important town house, comprising a central hall with a lateral fireplace and storeyed end rooms. Around 1600 the hall was floored over and an inserted attic now hides the impressive arch-braced roof timbers. The interior is all bare stonework (some re-used Roman masonry), dark oak beams and dressed stone doors and windows. Not far away is the Hanbury Arms, another late medieval lateral chimney house, incorporating the remains of Caerleon Castle *(OS map ref: 340 906)*.

Colwyn Bay *Penrhyn Old Hall*

The sizeable manor of the Pugh family is now a public house and restaurant beside a caravan park. The family chapel is in ruins close by. The oldest part of the stone house is

Cutaway view of Ty Mawr, Gwyddelwern, c.1600. Note the mix of stone and timber framing and the unusual form of the central roof truss

the left-hand wing, marked with a tall lateral chimney and diagonal stack, dating from the earl sixteenth century. The main first-floor chamber has painted murals on the plastered partition walls. To this was added a kitchen wing around 1590 with stepped gables characteristic of local gentry architecture *(OS map ref: SH 816 815).*

Gwyddelwern *Ty Mawr*
Thanks to restoration work, this late sixteenth-century pub is now one of the crowning glories of timber-framed architecture in Wales. Experts stripped away layers of wallpaper, plaster and rendering to reveal an almost intact framework with complex and lavishly decorated infill panels. Even more unsuspected was the fact that the ground floor had stone walls while the upper was timber-framed (rather like **Aberconwy House**). It was built in 1570-72 to a hearth-passage plan, comprising an outer room, cross-passage, hall, and twin inner rooms, all separated by post-and-panel partitions. A large stone fireplace perhaps replaced an original timber smoke-bay. The first floor is now one long room used as a restaurant, with massive oak rafters and a central hammer-beam style truss. Altogether an impressive and fascinating building, and a clear reminder of the benefits of sympathetic renovation *(OS map ref: SJ 075 467).*

Llangibby *The White Hart*
Prominently sited next to the Usk road, this is a classic example of the unit-system – two self-contained dwellings built corner to corner (see plan on p.79). They were built between 1580 and 1640; the first has a hearth-passage plan and the second a lobby-entrance. Each had a hall and inner room, but the partitions have since been removed. Inside there are massive stone fireplaces with corner winding stairs and some decorative plasterwork on the first floor *(OS map ref: ST 373 966).*

Llanfihangel Crucorney *The Skirrid Inn*
Often claimed to be the oldest pub in Wales (it actually dates from *c.*1650-80), the Skirrid is a splendid example of a Renaissance centrally-planned house. There are large rooms on either side of a central entrance passage, which leads through to a huge wooden staircase at the back (once used as a gallows according to legend). The symmetry of the façade has been significantly altered by later re-fenestration *(OS map ref: SO 326 207).*

Newtown *The Buck Inn*
The Buck Inn is one of the few survivors of timber-framed Newtown, though it is now sandwiched between modern buildings. Originally this seventeenth-century lobby-entry house was much larger, with a central chimney and a jettied upper floor, but some of the details have been lost in subsequent redevelopment. The Renaissance rear stairwell probably replaced a much smaller stair beside the hall fireplace *(OS map ref: SO 108 915).*

Penarth *Baron's Court*

This early sixteenth-century stone manor house was the home of the Herbert family and the arms of Sir George adorn the storeyed porch leading to the cross-passage. Much of the internal arrangement has survived and consists of service rooms, great hall with lateral fireplace and a long rear wing added around 1550. Although there have been later alterations many original details, including the carved stone doors and windows, survive *(OS map ref: ST 174 727)*.

Presteigne *The Radnorshire Arms*

A glorious timber-framed building of hearth-passage plan dated 1616, with the typical Renaissance details of a storeyed porch and clustered chimneys set diagonal rather than square. Some of the rooms have dark panelled walls, reputedly damaged in the past by treasure hunters. There is a large stair at the back of the entrance passage, but the rear has been altered by later extensions *(OS map ref: SO 314 644)*.

The Radnorshire Arms, Presteigne

Bibliography and further reading

Prehistoric, Roman & Dark Age:
J. Alcock, *Life in Roman Britain*. (Batsford/English Heritage 1996)
C.J. Arnold, J.L. Davies, *Roman and Early Medieval Wales*. (Sutton Publishing 2000)
G. Bedoyere, *The Buildings of Roman Britain*. (Batsford 1991)
G. Bedoyere, *Roman Towns in Britain*. (Batsford / English Heritage 1992)
R.J. Brewer, *Caerwent*. (CADW guidebook 1993)
C.J. Houlder, *Wales: An Archaeological Guide*. (Faber & Faber 1974)
F. Lynch, J. Davies, S. Green, *Prehistoric Wales*. (Sutton Publishing 2000)
T.J. O'Leary, K Blockley, C Musson, *Pentre Farm, Flint*. (BAR monograph 1989)
J. Manley, S. Grenter, F. Gale, *The Archaeology of Clwyd*. (Clwyd County Council 1991)
J. Percival, *The Roman Villa*. (Batsford 1976)
M. Reid, *Prehistoric Houses in Britain*. (Shire Archaeology 1993)
M. Redknap, *Vikings in Wales*. (National Museum of Wales 2000)
D. Robinson, *South Glamorgan's Heritage*. (Glamorgan-Gwent Archaeological Trust 1985)

Medieval & later:
A. Emery, *The Greater Medieval Houses of England & Wales*. (Cambridge University Press 2000)
C. Fox and Lord Raglan, *Monmouthshire Houses*. (National Museum of Wales 1951, 1953 & 1954)
H. Hughes & H.L. North, *The Old Cottages of Snowdonia*. (1908)
G. Nash, *Timber-framed buildings in Wales*. (NMW 1995)
I.C. Peate, *The Welsh House*. (revised ed. The Brython Press 1944)
P. Smith, *Houses of the Welsh Countryside*. (HMSO 1975 & 1988).
R. Suggett, *House & History in the March of Wales*. (RCAHMW 2005)
K. Roberts (ed.), *Lost farmsteads, deserted rural settlements in Wales*. (CBA 2006)
C.J. Williams & C. Kightly, *Nantclwyd y dre*. (Denbigh County Council 2007)
E. Wiliam, *Home Made Homes, dwellings of the rural poor in Wales*. (NMW 1988)
E. Wiliam, *Welsh Long-houses*. (University of Wales Press/NMW 1992)
M. Wood, *The English Medieval House*. (London 1965)

General:
R.W. Brunskill, *Traditional Buildings of Britain*. (Gollancz 1985)
R.W. Brunskill, *Vernacular Architecture, an illustrated handbook*. (Faber 2000)

J. Chambers, *The English House*. (Thames Methuen 1985)

P.R. Davis, *Historic Inns and Tavern of Wales & The Marches*. (Alan Sutton 1993)

J.B. Hilling, *The Historic Architecture of Wales*. (UWP 1976)

J.G. Jenkins, *Life and Tradition in Rural Wales*. (Alan Sutton 1976)

J. Jones, *Monmouthshire Wills 1560-1601*. (South Wales Record Society 1997)

J.G. Jones, *The Welsh Gentry 1536-1640*. (UWP 1998)

D.K. Leighton, *Mynydd Du and Fforest Fawr*. (RCAHMW 1997)

T. Lloyd, *The Lost Houses of Wales*. (Save Britain's Heritage 1986)

D.H. Owen (ed), *Settlement and Society in Wales*. (UWP 1989)

National Trust guidebook to Ty Mawr (various contributors 1988).

CADW guidebooks to Ancient and Historic Wales: *Glamorgan & Gwent*, E. Whittle (HMSO 1992); *Gwynedd*, F. Lynch (1995); *Clwyd & Powys*, H. Burnham (1995); *Dyfed*, S. Rees (1992).

Penguin guides to the architecture of Wales: *Clwyd*, E. Hubbard (1986); *Glamorgan*, J. Newman (1995); *Gwent*, J. Newman (2000); *Powys*, R. Haslam (1979).

Royal Commission on Ancient & Historical Monuments for Wales (RCAHMW) Inventories for the shires of: *Anglesey* (1937), *Caernarfon* (1954, 1960, 1962), *Glamorgan* (Vol IV part 1 1981, part 2 1988), *Brecon* (part 1, 1997).

Periodicals:

Archaeologia Cambrensis (Cambrian Archaeological Association)

Archaeology in Wales (Council for British Archaeology)

The Bulletin of the Board of Celtic Studies / Studia Celtica

Vernacular Archaeology (Vernacular Archaeology Group)

In addition to the above, further information on old houses can be found in the yearly journals of regional historical societies, such as the *Transactions of the Radnorshire Society* (particularly the volumes for 1968-73) and *Brycheiniog* (1963-69).

Index

Page numbers in italics refer to illustrations

Ty-mawr settlement, Holyhead 25-26
Ty Mawr, Castle Caereinion *xi*, *42*, 43, 50-51, *51*
Ty Mawr, Gwyddelwern *118*, 119
Ty Mawr, Wybrnant 75, 90, 114, *114*
Tynewydd, the Rhondda 82-84, *82*, *83*, *84*
ty unnos 93-94

unit system 79-80
Usk 17
upper-crucks 40

vernacular 2, 3
    Archaeology Group 5
Vikings 31-32
wattle and daub 15, 40-41

Welshpool 81
White Hart, the, Llangibby, near Usk 79, *79*, 119
Whitton, Llancarfan 21
wood 38, 39
Wrexham 81
Wynn, Robert 98

Also from Logaston Press

The Architecture of Death — Neolithic Chambered Tombs in Wales
by George Nash

An introductory chapter provides an overview of human migration and settlement in Wales leading to the creation of megalithic tombs. The 100 tombs with significant remains are grouped in eight core areas: around the Black Mountains; South-East Wales around Newport; the Gower Peninsula; South-West Wales; Harlech; the Lleyn Peninsula; Anglesey; and North Wales. A brief overview is given to each group as to similarities of style and approach to construction and/or use, and each site is described and what is known through excavation etc. set out. George Nash is a part-time lecturer at the Department of Archaeology and Anthropology, University of Bristol and a Principal Archaeologist at Giffords.

Paperback, 256 pages, 250 black and white illns, plans & maps,
ISBN 978 1904396338, Price: £17.50

The Celtic Christian Sites of the central and southern Marches
by Sarah & John Zaluckyj

Introductory chapters detail the arrival of Christianity in Britain and its early nature and style. The philosophy behind what became the Celtic brand of Christianity is discussed and biographical details given of saints who had contact with the area covered. The nature of a llan is described, as are the features often considered to indicate early Christian sites: holy wells, yew trees, circular and/or raised churchyard enclosures, and the Christianisation of pagan sites denoted by barrows or yews. This sets the scene for looking in detail at the 168 sites covered in the gazetteer, 21 in Montgomeryshire, 28 in Radnorshire, 42 in Breconshire, 30 in Herefordshire (that part which was the kingdom of Erging) and 47 in Gwent. Sarah & John Zaluckyj are bookdealers who live near the Welsh border and have also written: *Mercia – the Anglo-Saxon kingdom of central England* – also published by Logaston Press.

Paperback, 448 pages, with some 250 photographs,
ISBN 978 1904396574, Price: £12.95

Also from Logaston Press

Around & About South-West Wales
by Graham Roberts

Ten road-based tours cover Pembrokeshire, Cardiganshire, Carmarthenshire, parts of Glamorgan and a large part of Powys. Starting from seven different localities the tours cover a range of spectacular scenery, many well and less well known historically or architecturally interesting buildings, several towns, a good handful of villages, many beaches, a clutch of prehistoric sites, gardens open to the public, nature reserves and much besides. Ranging from 25 to 100 miles in distance, the tours are on a mixture of A and B roads and country lanes. Each tour starts with a flavour of what is included, followed by detailed route information as the tour unfolds, with information given on the notable sights that can be either seen from the road as you pass, or where you can stop to enjoy what is on offer. Graham Roberts was the City Surveyor for Hereford for many years, but his and his wife's origins lie in Wales and it is their knowledge of south-west Wales that has been used to compile this book.

Paperback, 288 pages with 300 black and white photographs ,
ISBN 978 1904396741, Price: £12.95

The Glaciations of Wales and Adjacent Areas
Colin A. Lewis & Andrew E. Richards (editors)

Fifteen leading geographers and quaternary scientists present the latest information on the quaternary development of Wales, the Cheshire-Shropshire lowlands, Severn valley, South West Peninsula, the east coast of Ireland and the Irish Sea and adjoining Celtic Sea basins. Intended for both the general reader who is interested in the physical environment and specialists, the book should enable university and senior school students, especially of geography, environmental science, and geology, to gain a sound appreciation of the evolution of the glaciated landscapes of Wales and surrounding areas. Colin A. Lewis, B.A., Ph.D. is Professor of Geography at Rhodes University in South Africa, and formerly lectured at University College Dublin. Andrew E. Richards, B.Sc., Ph.D., submitted his Ph.D. thesis on the Pleistocene stratigraphy of Herefordshire. He has lectured at the Universities of London, Limerick and at University College Worcester.

Paperback, 240 pages, 100 black and white photos, drawings, plans & tables,
ISBN 978 1904396369, Price: £25

Also from Logaston Press

The Monuments in the Landscape Series

This series covers prehistoric sites and castles on a county basis. Introductory sections cover the history and culture of the period, and then a comprehensive gazetteer includes the Monuments that remain. Those volumes in print:

Neolithic Sites of Cardiganshire, Carmarthenshire & Pembrokeshire
by George Children & George Nash, 148 pages, 84 illustrations, ISBN 978 1823827994, Price: £7.95

Prehistoric Sites of Montgomeryshire
by Beth McCormack, 176 pages, 80 illustrations, ISBN 978 1904396321, Price: £7.95

Castles and Bishops Palaces of Pembrokeshire
by Lise Hull, 240 pages, over 100 photos and plans, ISBN 978 1904396314, Price: £7.95

Castles of Glamorgan *by* Lise Hull
256 pages, around 100 illustrations, ISBN 978 1904396758, Price: £7.95

Castles of Breconshire
by Paul Remfry, 196 pages, 50 photos, maps & plans, ISBN 978 1873827802, Price: £8.95

Prehistoric Sites of Breconshire
by George Children & George Nash, 192 pages, 100 illustrations, ISBN 978 1873827574, Price: £7.95

Also from Logaston Press

Artisan Art: Vernacular wall paintings in the Welsh Marches, 1550-1650
by Kathryn Davies

Many ordinary people in the late sixteenth and early seventeenth centuries had art in their homes – not the high art of easel paintings but a form of rough and ready art painted on their walls. This book looks at what this decoration was, how it was done and its significance for those commissioning it. Kathryn Davies has researched vernacular buildings throughout the Welsh Marches and discovered extensive painted decoration in houses surviving from this period. They reveal the ways in which people hoped to impress their friends and neighbours, for wall paintings were a status symbol in their day just as houses and cars are today. This book will appeal to art historians and those interested in social history and vernacular architecture as well as serving as a reference book; a gazetteer includes photographs of almost all the paintings, and a map shows where in the Marches they are to be found (most of them in private houses not generally open to the public). Dr Davies studied vernacular architecture at Manchester University and completed a doctorate at Oxford University. She is currently a Historic Buildings Inspector with English Heritage.

240 pages with 312 mainly colour plates.
ISBN 978 1904396932 Hardback £24; ISBN 978 1904396925 Paperback £17.50

The Fitzalans, Earls of Arundel and Surrey, Lords of the Welsh Marches (1267-1415)
by Michael Burtscher

The Fitzalans ruled over estates in Sussex, Surrey, and Norfolk and were also powerful lords in the Welsh Marches where they tangled with the Mortimers and Owain Glyn Dŵr. Two of them were beheaded for treason: Earl Edmund, a staunch supporter of King Edward II, was executed at the hands of Queen Isabella and Roger Mortimer, while Earl Richard III, who became embroiled with King Richard II for his role as one of the Lords Appellant in the 1380s, was similarly condemned. The careers of the five earls are considered here, along with the management of their estates and their financial dealings. Many of the castles they built can still be seen, not least Arundel Castle and its gothic Fitzalan Chapel, but also many of their Marcher castles: Chirk, Oswestry, Clun and the ruins of Holt and Shrawardine. The family is also associated with Haughmond Abbey near Shrewsbury. Michael Burtscher was raised in Bellinzona, Switzerland, and holds degrees in medieval history from the Sorbonne and Oxford University. In researching this book he read largely unstudied original documents relating to the Fitzalan family.

Paperback, 192 pages with 52 black and white illustrations,
ISBN 978 1904396949 , Price: £12.95